railway

Identity, design and culture

Keith Lovegrove

Laurence King Publishing

LAURENCE KING

Published in 2004 by
Laurence King Publishing Ltd
71 Great Russell Street
London WC1B 3BN
T +44 20 7430 8850
F +44 20 7430 8880
E enquiries@laurenceking.co.uk
www.laurenceking.co.uk

A catalogue record for this book is available from the British Library.

ISBN 1 85669 407 0

Printed in China

PAGE 1 Audrey Hepburn's diminutive chic contrasts with the grandiose magnificence of a French SNCF 232U steam locomotive. On location for the film *Funny Face*, 1957.

FRONTISPIECE The Kyushu Railway Company's Tsubame 800 Series travels between Hakata and Kagoshina in 2 hours and 10 minutes. The Shinkansen combines state-of-the-art materials and production techniques with traditional materials and craftsmanship: camphor wood panels, wooden window blinds and *igusa* rush curtains in the washrooms are used to reflect Kyushu's natural environment.

6 Introduction

8 HARDWARE Industrial and interior design

80 SERVICE Cafés, dining cars and provisioning

118 IDENTITY Branding, livery and promotion

156 Acknowledgements

157 Picture credits and Bibliography

158 Index

The locomotive has shaped and parted nations, tamed wildernesses and built empires. Populations of vast metropoli and isolated communities have socialized and cross-polinated with the help of the two rails that never meet. In 1825, there were only 40 kilometres (25 miles) of public railway track in the world and it belonged to the Stockton & Darlington Railway in the north of England. A few years later, Stephenson's steam-powered Rocket ran at an unprecedented speed of 50 kilometres (31 miles) per hour prompting sceptics to warn that the human body could not withstand or ultimately survive such speeds. Today, with the benefit of a magnetic contact-free levitating princple, the high-speed Maglev skims across the landscape at 500 kilometres per hour and over 1 million kilometres of railway track spans the planet – enough to circumnavigate the globe 28 times. In almost two centuries of rail history, countless railway companies have chased fortunes and misfortunes – mergers and acquisitions have followed successes and bankruptcies. Locomotives christened with numerals, royalty, legendary heroes and Roman gods have been powered by steam, diesel and electricity (and even dynamite) and designed with form and function and sometimes with fashion in mind. On the inside, passenger accommodation ranges from the tasteless and the tasteful to opulent luxury and designer-minimalism. This book illustrates the identity, design and culture of the passenger train through the work of the catering and services departments, branding consultants, and industrial designers – and their pursuit to create the ultimate in train travel.

HARDWARE

Industrial and interior design

GREAT

Sceptics and radical protesters were there from the start of passenger rail travel. Fears about whether the human body would endure the high speeds of 50 kilometres (30 miles) per hour and above led some to suggest that the head and torso would simply explode. Predictions of carnage were made by cartoonists in national newspapers, and English farmers, anticipating an explosion of rail traffic through the countryside, feared for the fertility of their livestock.

While the debate raged, others were busy with invention. Activity in science and engineering was changing Britain's literal and social landscape in the mid-eighteenth century, as the Industrial Revolution began. Advances in the textile and iron industries meant an increase in the demand for power; static steam engines were used to pump water out of mines and to haul coal from their dark, noxious depths. Engineer Richard Trevithick developed a number of high-pressure steam engines for the Cornish and Welsh mining industries. He also began experimenting with steam locomotion and, by 1796, had produced a miniature locomotive. A few years later, a much larger version, which he named Puffing Devil, was able to carry a few passengers on short journeys. Trevithick's creativity was a classic case of 'genius before his time' and, despite further successes with the Penydarren in 1804 (the world's first steam locomotive to carry fare-paying passengers) and his Catch Me Who Can locomotives, financial backing was not forthcoming, so he had to rely on his expertise with static steam engines driving the factories of the Industrial Revolution to secure a living. Short-sightedness on the part of the government, coupled with the British propensity to drive home-grown innovation abroad, led Trevithick to travel as far as South America to develop his unique ideas. Although his pioneering creations will forever represent the birth of the locomotive, Richard Trevithick died unrecognized and in poverty at the Bull Inn in Dartford, England, in 1833.

PREVIOUS PAGES 46 m (150 ft) beneath the seabed Eurostar speeds through 50 km (31 miles) of Channel Tunnel in 20 minutes. The $15 billion tunnel consists of 3 interconnected tubes: 1 rail track each way plus 1 service tunnel. 153 km (95 miles) of tunnels were dug by nearly 13,000 engineers, and technicians; the rubble removed from the tunnel has increased the size of Britain by 36 ha (90 acres).

TOP The domed-head rivets so indicative of the construction of Victorian locomotives.

ABOVE The 1.75 m (5 ft, 9 in) diameter wheels are the driving force for 196 tons of KF-1 class steam locomotive built in 1935, now resting at the National Railway Museum, York, UK.

FACING The Rocket was designed by father and son George and Robert Stephenson and built by Robert Stephenson & Son in 1829. It became famous by winning the Rainhill Trials; a competition held to establish the most efficient locomotive for railway haulage. Its success and that of the Liverpool and Manchester Railway on which it ran for 7 years led to steam railways being established across Europe. This photograph, taken in 1876, is one of the earliest in existence, taken outside the Patent Office Museum in South Kensington, London which was the precursor to the Science Museum.

ABOVE AND FAR RIGHT The owner of the Green carriage hired a French upholsterer who created a full-size set to present his design for approval before it was transferred to the carriage itself. Every item of furniture was slightly reduced in scale to maximize space yet still accommodate human requirements. The carriage is now on show at the California State Railroad Museum, Sacramento, USA.

RIGHT The interior of Monterey & Salinas Valley coach-baggage car No 1 built in 1874, also at the California State Railroad Museum.

FACING TOP The private train car Alexander was built in 1890 by the Pullman Palace Car Building Company of Illinois, for A.A.McLeod, President of the Philadelphia and Reading Railway.

FACING LEFT Interior of an early Pullman railroad car.

FACING RIGHT In 1825 there were only 40 km (25 miles) of public railway track in the world and it belonged to the Stockton & Darlington Railway. This photograph shows a first-class carriage of a Stockton & Darlington passenger train.

ABOVE Off to the USA: Fireman Blackett of the London Midland & Scottish Railway saying farewell to his workmates and officials at Carlisle before finishing duty. He is off to America to assist on the Royal Scot which is touring the USA after appearing at the Century of Progress World's Fair in Chicago, in 1933.

FACING The London Midland & Scottish Railway streamlined locomotive Duchess of Gloucester leaves Euston Station in London on her first long-distance journey. Designed by Sir William Stainer, the Duchess of Gloucester was put to traffic in May 1938, the first of the class to carry the LMS Crimson Lake livery.

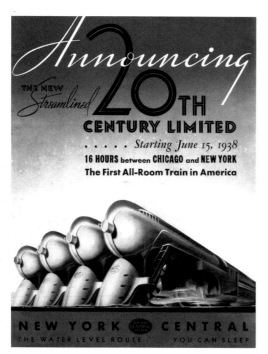

ABOVE AND FACING Henry Dreyfuss's magnificent Art Deco-style 20th Century Limited streamlined locomotive of 1938. The J-3a class Hudsons were built by the Alco (American Locomotive Company) for New York Central's Water Level Route. The vertical nose fin that bisects the headlight and culminates at the skyline-casing air intake, doubles as the fastening of clamshell doors; bolts through the fin held the doors secure until servicing access to the smokebox was required. Streamlining revolutionized the look and, to a lesser extent, the performance of steam locomotives in the 1930s, with industrial designers such as Otto Kuhler, Walter Dorwin Teague, Norman Bel Geddes, Raymond Loewy, Paul Cret and Henry Dreyfuss leading the way.

ABOVE RIGHT 1937: streamlined steam-powered I-5 class locomotive engine built by the Baldwin Locomotive Works for the New York, New Hampshire and Hartford Railroad. Otherwise known as the Shore Liners, the locomotive was described by the railroad as a 'modern high-speed rifle bullet' – an exaggeration perhaps, although the streamliner covered the 253 km (157 miles) between Boston and New Haven with 2 stops en route in under 3 hours.

Conversely, pomp and circumstance were the order of the day at the Rainhill Trials, held just outside Liverpool in 1829, and publicity was certainly the intention of the directors of the Liverpool & Manchester Railway. Engineers, scientists, royalty and interested officials from the government were among the spectators. The challenge offered by the rail company was for a locomotive to pull a load on their soon-to-be-completed track with the greatest speed and the least expense. Among the specific conditions that had to be met in order to secure the £500 prize were that each engine entered in the competition should weigh no more than 6 tons, be capable of towing carriages equal to three times the weight of the engine itself and travel at a speed of at least 16 kilometres (10 miles) per hour. Other stipulations included a height limit of 4.5 metres (15 feet) (including chimney), a maximum boiler steam pressure of 50 pounds per square inch and that the engine should 'effectually consume its own smoke'. The curb on pollution was for the comfort of passengers.

Of the ten original entrants, only five actually took part. The portion of the rail line chosen for the trials lay on the Manchester side of Rainhill Bridge, about 14.5 kilometres (9 miles) from Liverpool, where the track ran level for approximately 3.2 kilometres (2 miles). Cutting a dash with its distinctive yellow-and-black livery and white chimney stack, Robert Stephenson's Rocket was the first engine to perform, and, despite a great 'inequality in its velocity', it drew over 12 tons at a rate of over 16 kilometres (10 miles) per hour. Further trials, including the drawing of a carriage containing 25 excited passengers, proved the Rocket to be the unrivalled winner. The power of the media, however, may have helped the judges come to their decision; *The Mechanics Magazine*, a weekly publication, followed the trials closely, reporting in its Saturday, October 17th issue that 'The directors of the Liverpool and Manchester Railway cannot do wrong in awarding Mr Stephenson a premium of £500 for producing an

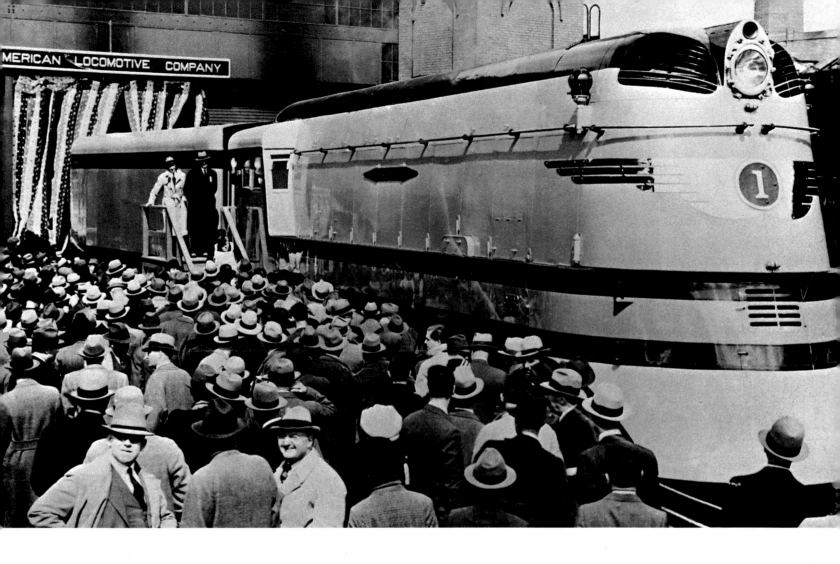

ABOVE Dozens of curious spectators attend the dedication of the Milwaukee Road's Hiawatha No 1 on April 30, 1935, at the American Locomotive Company works in New York. The oil-fuelled, steam-driven locomotive could attain speeds of 193 km (120 miles) an hour. Industrial designer Otto Kuhler's distinctive shovel-nosed bathtub shroud was a departure from the bullet-nosed designs of his contemporaries. The Atlantic class in bright orange, maroon and black livery cut a dash as it sped west out of the Schenectady works.

RIGHT Industrial designer Raymond Loewy poses on his streamlined Pacific K4 with an unshrouded K4 on the track behind. Altoona Works, Pennsylvania Railroad, 1936.

FACING Spaciousness, suggesting a modern split-level living room, marked the appearance of the Pennsylvania Railroad's new tubular train built by the Budd Company in 1956. The stainless-steel lightweight passenger coach accumulated 20 years and 3 million km (almost 2 million miles) in service. The coaches were low with a step-down center section made possible by moving the air-conditioning equipment from under the floor, hence the elevated end sections. There are reclining seats for 56 passengers in the main section, and for twelve beyond.

ABOVE The comparative light weight of the diesel-powered, streamlined Burlington Zephyr is tested using manpower supplied by the tug-of-war team of E.G. Budd, the makers of the train. Philadelphia, Pennsylvania, 1934. The Chicago Burlington and Quincy Railroad set out to revolutionize passenger rail service and president, Ralph Budd joined forces with Edward Budd (no relation), an autobody manufacturer from Philadelphia. Ralph Budd sought improvements in speed and efficiency – and also appearance – with the help of architects Paul Cret and Holabird & Root; Edward Budd brought this vision to life with his innovative use of stainless steel and streamlining. At the same time, Charles Kettering of General Motors was experimenting to perfect the diesel locomotive engine. Inspecting the efficient and reliable engine at the 1933 Chicago World's Fair, Ralph Budd recognized this as the engine that would propel his lightweight train.

FACING The minimalist interior of the Burlington Zephyr now on view at the Museum of Science and Industry in Chicago.

engine which has done what no locomotive engine ever before accomplished – gone seventy miles continuously, at an average rate of about twelve miles an hour, with a load of three times its own weight attached to it: which has realized a degree of speed and power, which, though much desired, had scarcely been anticipated even by the most sanguine.' Whatever the impact of the spin, the spectators lining the temporary grandstands at the Rainhill Trials over those few autumnal days were aware that they were witnessing not only a transport revolution, but also the acceleration of social, cultural and economic change for Britain and the rest of the world.

During the 'Golden Age' of steam, engineering dictated form and, by extension, aesthetics. The defining visual characteristics of the steam locomotive are a collective accident of design. From the buffers to the trailing tender, the elements of the driving force are all on view – the boiler, cylinders, coupling rods and driving wheels embody the architecture of the machine. Product design of the Industrial Revolution was executed by locomotive builders and engineers. Understandably, the elegance of innovation is not the first concern of the pioneering engineer; such considerations as performance and durability are far more important than the delicacies of style and 'good looks'. This is not to say that early steam engines are unattractive vehicles. Indeed, most have a well-proportioned majesty. Styling was dictated by weight, strength and engineering efficiency; iron plates, accented with rows of dome-headed rivets on the periphery, were an essential adornment. Decorative elements were limited to a filigreed crown on the smoke stack or a polished brass dome on the firebox; the *beauty* of Victorian engineering was its exoskeletal and random styling.

By the mid-nineteenth century, production of steam locomotives reached the hundreds, and advances in engineering brought about a metamorphosis in the appearance of engines. The inclined and

ABOVE LEFT The Mardi Gras theme is employed in the parlour car of Illinois Central's Panama Limited, 1942.

BELOW LEFT Rough-hewn outpost called The Frontier Shack. The bar is equipped with a 'vintage' spiggot dispensing draught beer from kegs situated in the storage room behind the bar. The baggage tavern cars were built by Pullman-Standard for Union Pacific's City of Denver trains in 1936.

FACING Linear aluminium, tubular chrome chair frames and dark leather couchettes complement one another in the lounge bar of the Denver Zephyr, 1936.

vertical cylinders that had been a distinctive feature of early experimental models were now mounted horizontally and hidden from view next to the multi-tubular boiler. Single pairs of driving wheels were substituted with multiple, coupled pairs, with smaller carrying wheels to the front and rear. While Robert Stephenson & Company were still at the forefront of manufacturing in England, an ardent competitive spirit was thriving. Engineering innovations, such as spring axles and fully water-jacketed firebox casings, together with the rearrangement of elements, created the shape of the new.

At the leading end of locomotive technology, engineers were improving steam pressure and tractive effort, while developing conjugated valve-gears. Engines built by Alco, Baldwin and Lima were powering America's railroads, which consisted of almost 161,000 kilometres (100,000 miles) of track at the beginning of the twentieth century. Worldwide, hundreds of railroad companies were enticing passengers with their, often luxurious, facilities and with the promise of faster schedules. Design, engineering and new materials converged with vigorous commercial enterprise to respond to the demands of flocking rail passengers, while, to some extent, creating those very demands.

The design of passenger cars drawn by the early American locomotives, such as the De Witt Clinton, built by the West Point Foundry for the Mohawk & Hudson line in 1831, was basic – the carriages were, essentially, stagecoaches. Each four-wheeled unit accommodated up to four passengers inside, with more exposed seating on the roof for a further four travellers, plus luggage. The coaches were suspended on leaf springs, and the ride, though undoubtedly smoother than that offered by their horse-drawn precursors, with their frequent encounters with potholes, was comparable to being in an oversized perambulator. They were more comfortable, however, than the earlier open, cattle-truck style of third-class cars (standing room only). The rapid expansion of passengers, as a form of profitable 'freight',

FACING TOP The Skytop observation car of the Milwaukee Road's Hiawatha at the Milwaukee Depot, Minneapolis, Minnesota in 1948. The multi-faceted dome was the finishing touch of industrial designer Brook Stevens, who was also responsible for streamlining the Studebaker and the Harley Davidson.

FACING BELOW An earlier Hiawatha observation lounge brought up the rear on the A-class Atlantic type. The fins above the windows provided shade as well as accenting the futuristic look of the exterior; and on the inside the Tip Top Tap lounge car was the most popular spot on the train, rivalling the best clubs in Chicago, 1937.

ABOVE Airship designer Franz Kruckenberg's Schienenzeppelin (Rail Zeppelin), held the world's speed record on rails for 20 years – of 230 km (143 miles) an hour. The silver-gray locomotive travelled 257 km (160 miles) between Hamburg and Smandou, a suburb of Berlin, in 1 hour and 36 minutes, reaching the highest speed shortly after its departure and making an average speed of about 171 km (106 miles) an hour. The 'Zep on wheels' seated fifty persons and travelled four miles on a gallon of gasoline. A BMW airplane engine was used to power a wooden propeller that pushed the light-weight railcar through the air.

The failure of the Rail Zeppelin has been attributed to everything from the fears of the possible consequences of using an open propeller in crowded railway stations to competition between Kruckenberg's Flugbahngesell-schaft company and the Deutsche Reichsbahn's separate efforts to build a Fliegende Zuege. The Schienenzeppelin was, however, an important part of the evolution of high-speed passenger rail transport. Photographed here at the Stadion-Rennbahn Grunewald in Berlin, 1930.

ABOVE 'You're the smartest girl I ever spent the night with on the train.' remarks Roger Thornhill (Cary Grant) to an icy-cool blonde Eve Kendall (Eva Marie Saint) on board the 20th Century Limited from New York to Chicago in a scene from *North by Northwest*, 1959, directed by Alfred Hitchcock. The master of suspense was the most enthusiastic exponent of the train as cinematic mise en scène and was keen to unite couples in adventurous and amorous frisson in the confines of the railway compartment. In his *The 39 Steps* (1935), adapted from the John Buchan novel, he brings together an unsuspecting couple in an on-board clinch.

Hitchcock once again casts Cary Grant (as Johnnie Aysgarth) in the 1941 film *Suspicion*; he meets shy Lina McLaidlaw (Joan Fontaine) on a train whilst trying to travel in a first-class carriage with a third -class ticket (FACING BELOW LEFT).

Hitchcock's signature cameo appearances are often found in rail-related scenes – a man at London's Victoria Station in *The Lady Vanishes* (1938); a card player aboard a train to Santa Rosa in *Shadow of a Doubt* (1943); a passenger alighting a train with a cello in *The Paradine Case* (1947); and a man boarding a train with a double bass in *Strangers on a Train* (1951).

FACING ABOVE Entertainment on board the Great Northern's Empire Builder in 1947 includes conversation in the smoking lounge while gathered around the radio console. USA, 1947.

FACING RIGHT On-board movie. USA, 1920s.

meant that the carriage was soon to require the attentions of the engineer *and* the interior designer. Longer journeys and increased patronage inevitably lead to the development of the longer day coach.

The design and construction of early passenger cars, made almost entirely of wood with a steel rod-reinforced substructure, were carried out by the foundries and coach-builders. The number of apprentice wagon-makers and pattern-cutters burgeoned. One such apprentice, Theodore Tuttle Woodruff, eventually became Master Car Builder for the Terre Haute, Alton & St Louis Railroad of Illinois in 1855. A year later, he received two patents for a car seat that converted into a bed. A complicated arrangement of pivoted seat cushions produced a lower twin birth, almost at floor level, while a middle single birth incorporated a shelf-table. A hinged upper birth folded down from the wall at shoulder height. And so, ingeniously, a recumbent party of four required no more space than when seated. At bedtime, curtains were drawn between the lower births and in front of the upper one.

Woodruff's pioneering sleeping cars were a success on the New York Central line, and, by the end of 1858, eight of the midwestern railroads had adopted his patented carriages. Business boomed and Woodruff became principal stockholder of the Central Transportation Company. He enjoyed a long and successful career, which featured numerous, diverse inventions beyond carriage building, until, in an ironic twist of fate, he was knocked down and killed by a train, at the age of 81.

The Central Transportation Company eventually assigned most of its patent rights to the Pullman Palace Car Company. Luxury train travel was de rigeur in the late nineteenth century, and George Mortimer Pullman was the undisputed king of rail-car manufacturing. The 'hotel on wheels' was Pullman's concept. The rather basic sleeping cars that he had encountered as a travelling furniture contractor led him to experiment by acquiring two day coaches, to which he applied his ideas. Pullman

LEFT Locomotive 5926 of the Canadian Pacific Railway rests at Banff Station, Alberta, Canada, 1947. The majestic Castle Mountain dominates the background scenery. An almost identical view (ABOVE) is used as reference for an illustration on a timetable in 1960.

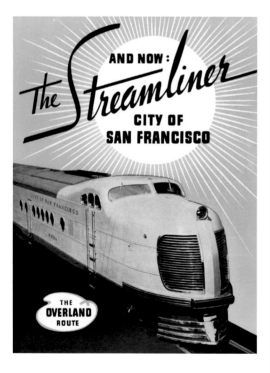

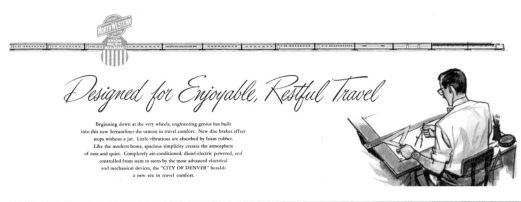

Designed for Enjoyable, Restful Travel

Beginning down at the very wheels, engineering genius has built into this new Streamliner the utmost in travel comfort. New disc brakes effect stops without a jar. Little vibrations are absorbed by foam rubber. Like the modern home, spacious simplicity creates the atmosphere of ease and quiet. Completely air-conditioned, diesel-electric powered, and controlled from stem to stern by the most advanced electrical and mechanical devices, the "CITY OF DENVER" heralds a new era in travel comfort.

new *Streamliner* "City of Denver"

BETWEEN CHICAGO AND DENVER

was confident that rail travellers were prepared to pay extra for comfort, and, therefore, planned the construction of an entirely new vehicle, the Pioneer. It cost over $20,000, five times more than an average railroad passenger car of the mid-1860s. He furnished it with polished black walnut, candelabras and marble washstands. Critics dismissed the result as extravagant, while moralists joined the tirade against such exotic, hedonistic shenanigans. It was deemed impractical, too, regarded by some as too large and heavy, and, thus, uneconomical. Morbidly, the assassination of President Abraham Lincoln saved the day for Pullman; the state of Illinois included the 'extravagant' carriage in the funeral procession, assuring the future of the Pioneer car and the prosperity of George M. Pullman. Sceptics underestimated the travelling public's readiness to pay more for luxury. The demand for Pullman's sleepers, parlour cars and diners over the next 15 years established the Pullman Palace Car Company as the world's largest manufacturer. Expansion lead Pullman to buy 1,460 hectares (3,600 acres) of land, just south of Chicago, resulting in America's first industrial estate.

Pullman frequently organized promotional tours – on one particular week-long land cruise, he published a daily newsletter, describing the brand new cars: 'The train leads off with a baggage car, the front of which has five large ice closets and a refrigerator for the storing of fruits, meats and vegetables. The balance of the car is for baggage, with the exception of a square in one corner, where stands a new quarto-medium Gordon press, upon which this paper is printed.' The copywriter goes on to describe the in-house, on-board graphic design studio. 'Next comes a very handsome smoking car, which is divided into four rooms. The first is the printing office, which is supplied with black walnut cabinets fitted with the latest styles of type for newspaper and job work.' Sumptuous facilities for passenger comfort and recreation included a wine room, hairdressing and shaving saloons, and a library. The publicity also

Union Pacific's first streamliner in 1934 was numbered M-10000 and was a three-car lightweight, articulated passenger train powered by an Electro-Motive Division 600-horsepower internal combustion engine. The train was one of the first internal combustion-powered passenger trains in America.

Separate diesel passenger locomotives (as opposed to complete articulated trains) began to appear with the arrival of the Union Pacific's third streamliner, M-10002, in 1936.

The Copper King lounge (FACING AND RIGHT) on board the 1938 City of Los Angeles M-10004, built by Pullman-Standard, sported a brushed copper finish on the side walls, heat pipes and frames of the round windows. Each of the 29 window panes were polarized and could be rotated 90 degrees by means of a crank to block out some of the sun's rays.

ABOVE AND FACING LEFT The Electro-Motive Division M-10004 featured an 'automobile-design' elevated cab.

TOP Literature promoting Union Pacific's luxurious Streamliner, City of Denver, 1954.

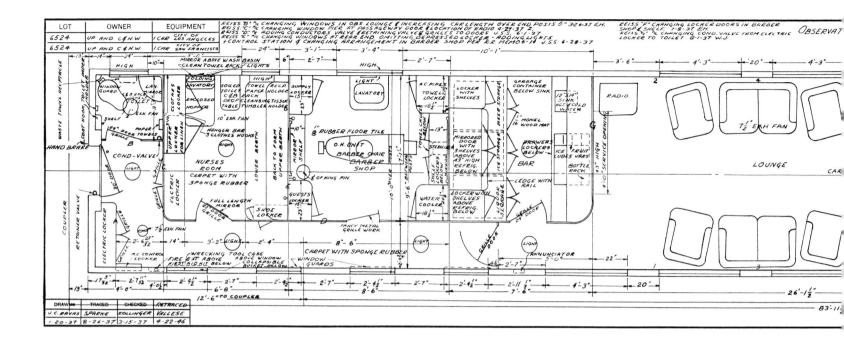

ABOVE The plan of the City of Los Angeles and the City of San Francisco as drawn by the Pullman-Standard Car Manufacturing Company, for delivery to the Union Pacific and the Chicago & North Western railroads. The plan was originally drawn in 1937 and retraced in 1946.

FACING LEFT Passengers tuck into an hors d'oeuvre of chilled seafood cocktail in front of a backdrop mural depicting a Hollywood production stage. Union Pacific, 1950s.

FACING RIGHT An advertisement for Chicago & North Western Railroad's Streamliners boasts the fastest routes from Chicago to the Pacific Coast and Colorado.

highlighted the latest technical innovations: 'The cars of this train are lighted during the night in a new and novel manner, there being under each an ingeniously constructed machine which produces from liquid hydrocarbon a gas equal in brilliancy to that made in the ordinary way.' It would be almost another 20 years before electric lighting would replace gas or kerosene lamps. At this time, the Pullman cars were heated by steam, piped from the locomotive, replacing the earlier wood-burning stoves.

Pullman became synonymous with luxury train travel in the USA and, in 1868, one particular foreign visitor to take a keen interest in such service was the creative, young Belgian, Georges Nagelmackers. The European sleeping-car industry at that time was at an embryonic stage, and Nagelmackers was convinced that a market existed for a Pullman-style luxury back home. His initial proposals met with a limp response from rail companies, and the enterprise looked doomed until he joined forces with American engineer Colonel William d'Alton Mann who provided financial support. Contracts with two train companies in France, and the patronage of the British Prince of Wales on a visit to Berlin, launched Nagelmackers's ambition of establishing an international service from Paris to Vienna. Expansion happened quickly, and two years later the Compagnie Internationale des Wagons-Lits et des Grands Express Européens was registered.

From the birth of the Orient Express in 1883, Nagelmackers's cars were to grace the international scene from Paris to Bucharest and, later, to Constantinople, via the Simplon tunnel at the Swiss–Italian border. The Wagons-Lits company also furnished the Trans-Siberian Express. The rail journey from Moscow to Manchuria took nine days and, to help the traveller while away the hours, a library of over 400 books in four languages was at hand. Chess sets were stocked for the competitive of spirit, and the dining car was open from breakfast at 7 o' clock in the morning to late supper at 11 o' clock at night.

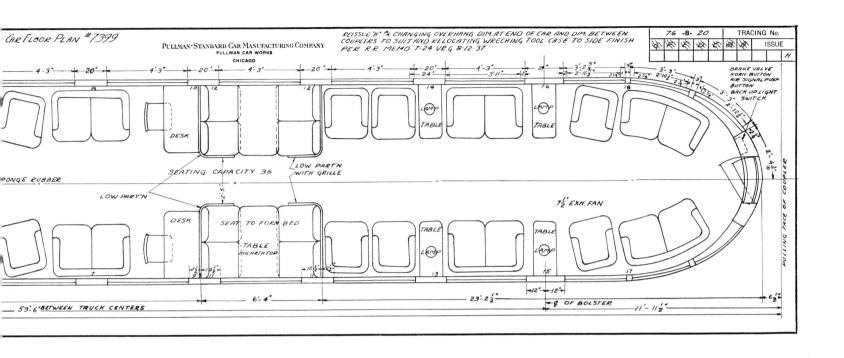

Car Floor Plan #7399

PULLMAN-STANDARD CAR MANUFACTURING COMPANY
PULLMAN CAR WORKS
CHICAGO

REISSUE "H" ½ CHANGING OVERHANG DIM. AT END OF CAR AND DIM. BETWEEN
COUPLERS TO SUIT AND RELOCATING WRECKING TOOL CASE TO SIDE FINISH
PER R.R. MEMO T-24 VR G 8-12-37

76 -B- 20 | TRACING No.
ISSUE | H

ABOVE Bar-side conversation, a round of whist and live music in the piano lounge bar on board Union Pacific, 1950s.

FACING Men's talk in the observation lounge on board Canadian Pacific, 1968.

The florid aesthetic of the French kings of the Bourbon Dynasty was all the rage at the start of the twentieth century, and Nagelmackers furnished two lounge cars in the style of Louis XV and Louis XVI to show in Paris at the prestigious World Exhibition of 1900. Windows were hung with rich, pink silk, and the plush, green upholstery of the chairs was complemented by gilt embellishments and highly carved woodwork. The ceilings were adorned with painted panels, depicting classical scenes of flora and fauna. The message was clear: the traveller need not leave behind the trappings of fashionable homes and luxury hotels.

By the late nineteenth century, styles were changing – the British Arts and Crafts movement was moving away from the liberal use of classical adornment of the previous century and by the early twentieth century, a fresh and very different design philosophy was to emerge out of the radical political and social change in Europe. The functional style of the Bauhaus, shunned in its native Germany by the Nazis, produced a practical synthesis of architecture and industrial design. Following a ten-year delay, due to the First World War, the Paris Exposition Internationale des Arts Décoratifs et Industriels Modernes was eventually held in 1925. The exhibition launched the Art Deco style, which attempted to present a cleaner and more modern aesthetic. A band of European emigrés took these new creative directions to the land of opportunity.

Graphic artist Otto Kuhler moved to the USA from Germany in 1923. His later conceptual drawings of new ideas for New York Central's Class J-1 4-6-4 Baltic locomotive (first built in 1927) secured him a career as an industrial designer, with subsequent commissions from the American Locomotive Company and others. Baltimore & Ohio appointed him Consulting Engineer of Design in 1937 to create a new interior for their Royal Blue, as well as to streamline the locomotive. Kuhler applied a consistent interior

ABOVE Taking advantage of the 'modern' electric razor facility in the men's washroom on board a Union Pacific train.

LEFT Chaos in the men's washroom in the hour before breakfast. The Great Northern Railway's Empire Builder, 1947.

FACING ABOVE Ladies in the washroom on board the Challenger Domeliner that offered a daily route between Chicago and Los Angeles, 1961.

FACING LEFT 'For the ladies...' as the 1956 El Capitan brochure explained, 'The lounge-dressing rooms for ladies in El Capitan chair cars are practically boudoirs on wheels. Each of these spacious rooms has large mirrors (and plenty of them), dressing tables, shelves, and lounge seats, as well as boudoir chairs. Comfortable, carefree clothes are the vogue of lady travelers on El Capitan, and with the spacious dressing rooms you can change as often as you like.'

FACING RIGHT A lady's maid in attendance on board the Great Northern Railway's Oriental Limited, 1926.

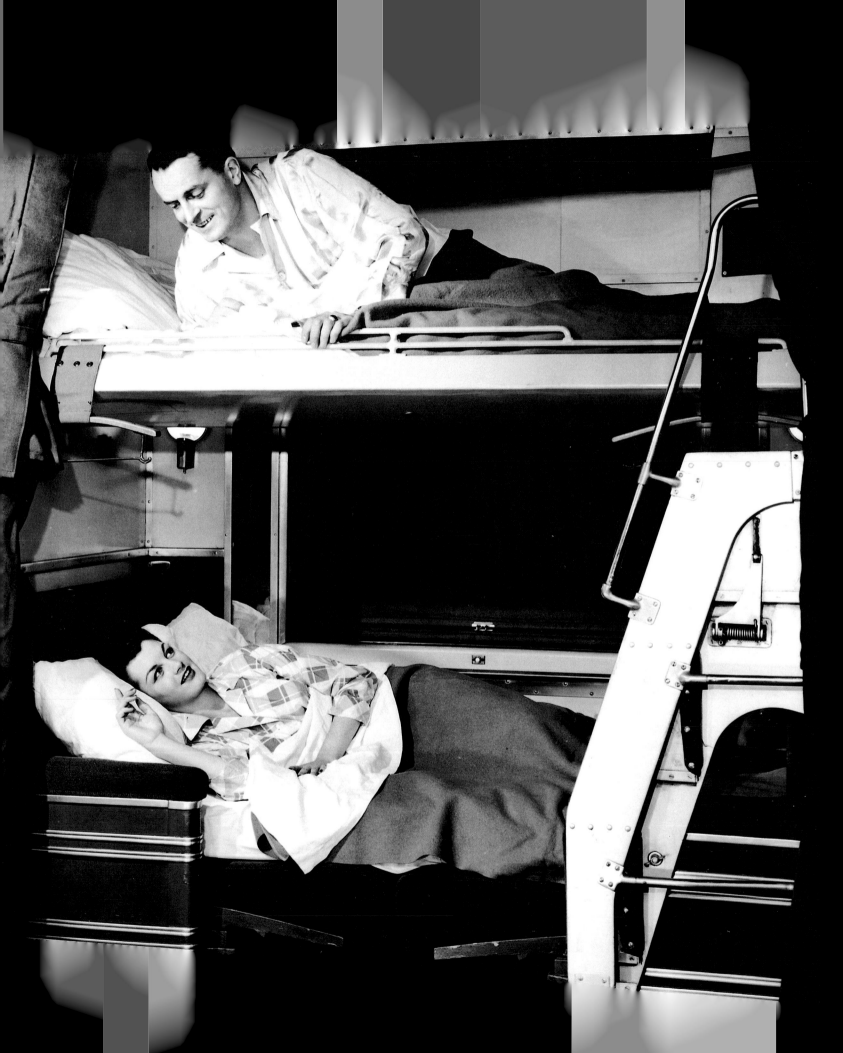

design scheme throughout the train. Further work, including the styling of the Lehigh Valley Railroad's Pacifics, which ran between Pittston, Philadelphia and New York City, illustrated that Kuhler understood how to lure passengers to become his clients through repackaging and streamlining. On the K-5s built by Baldwin in 1916 and restyled by Kuhler in 1938, he set the headlight in the centre of the Pacific's bullet-nosed cylinder shroud 'to suggest resemblance to an airplane'. Beneath the nose, he placed three bold, horizontal fins, which followed the curved contours that doubled as footholds for maintenance; stainless-steel handrails, which swooped up from the pilot guard, continued alongside the cylinder up to the chromium-plated window frames of the cab. The streamlining appealed to passengers, and more railroads saw the positive effect consulting creative draughtsmen had on ticket sales.

In May 1934, the Chicago, Burlington and Quincy Railroad's God of the West Wind hurtled east from Denver Union Station to Halstead Street, Chicago. On board, correspondents from the *Rocky Mountain News* and the *Chicago Tribune* (among others) helped document a seminal moment in rail travel. Motormen Ernie Weber, Jack Ford and Ernie Kuehn took it in turns to drive the Burlington Zephyr over 1,600 kilometres (1,000 miles) in just over 13 hours. The train's final destination that day was the shore of Lake Michigan, where it took its place among the display of futuristic transport at the Century of Progress exposition. New technology, both in the fabrication of the train and its motive power, was brought together with the creative skills of architects Paul Cret and Holabird & Root to deliver the unique result. The Budd Company used shotwelding, developed three years earlier, to construct the lightweight, corrugated, stainless-steel exterior and to secure it to the frame. The streamlined, three-car, articulated train was powered by a new diesel-electric engine, produced by the Electro-Motive Division of General Motors. The engine could convert up to 40 percent of the heat from burning fuel and, so, was

ABOVE Joe (Jack Lemmon), the saxophone player, is Josephine in an all-girls band that he joined with Jerry (Tony Curtis), the bass violin player, to be one step ahead of the mob after witnessing the 1929 St Valentine's Day Massacre in Chicago. Marilyn Monroe plays Sugar Kane Kowalczyk in Billy Wilder's *Some like It Hot* (1959). After a train ride that sets a record for the number of people in an upper berth, they arrive in Miami.

FACING Daytime chairs convert to sleeping berths with a folding ladder for access.

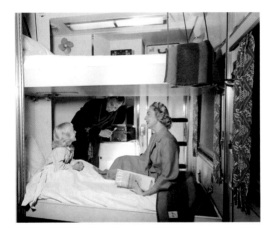

ABOVE Beds fold out of the wall in the Duplex-Roomette of the Chateau series car, Canadian Pacific Railway, 1954.

LEFT Time for bed on the Manor series sleeper of the Canadian Pacific Railway, 1954.

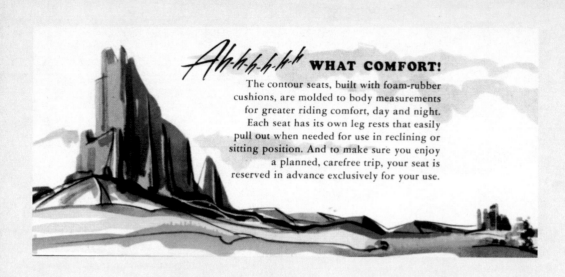

Ah-h-h-h-h WHAT COMFORT!

The contour seats, built with foam-rubber
cushions, are molded to body measurements
for greater riding comfort, day and night.
Each seat has its own leg rests that easily
pull out when needed for use in reclining or
sitting position. And to make sure you enjoy
a planned, carefree trip, your seat is
reserved in advance exclusively for your use.

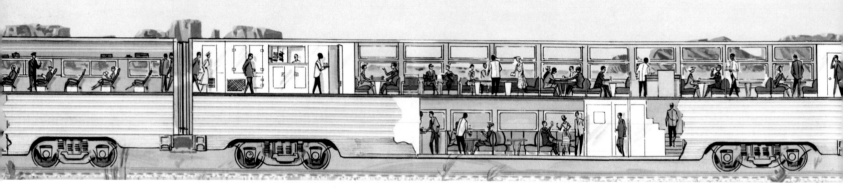

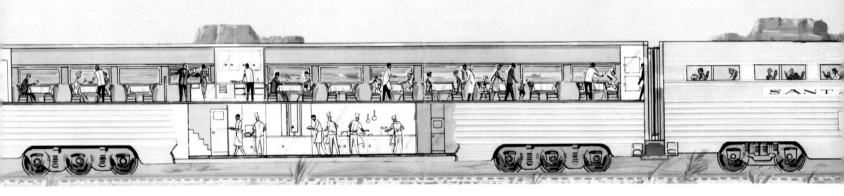

much more efficient than steam. Chicago, Burlington & Quincy engineers gave the train a low centre of gravity to handle the high speeds on curves, giving the impression of it hugging the tracks. The power car, with its gladiator-helmet visage, contained the eight-cylinder diesel engine and mail storage; the centre car combined a large baggage compartment with a small buffet section and 20 coach seats; the trailing car carried 40, plus 12 first-class passengers in the observation lounge. The interior was as sleek as the exterior; 'functional machine as art' was the design philosophy – naked stainless steel on the outside, and clean and simple decor on the inside. Indirect, fluorescent lighting, soothing pastels of warm grey and green, and tubular-aluminium seat frames, upholstered in leather, created the luxuriously modern environment. The Zephyr was the answer to the Chicago, Burlington & Quincy's undertaking to revolutionize their passenger rail service. In the first year of operation, the fastest, sleekest and most fuel-efficient train in existence increased the company's passenger traffic by over 50 percent, proving that innovative design, combined with sound technology, equals wise investment.

The New York Central System (NYCS) ran some of the most fashionable routes in the country. In 1935, they decided to upgrade their Cleveland-to-Detroit service to entice new passengers. Speed and reliability would be the marketing message, and, appropriately, the Roman god of commerce was plucked from mythology to provide the name. The Mercury project encountered a false start, as industrial designer Henry Dreyfuss's initial proposal for brand-new rolling stock was costed and rejected by the financial department. Dreyfuss resurrected the project following a train ride from his Manhattan office through the Bronx. He saw rows of unused commuter cars and persuaded NYCS's president that the surplus stock could be rebuilt to provide the winged-footed service. With recosting approved, Dreyfuss started work on streamlining the old K-5a Pacifics. Much streamlining of the 1930s

ABOVE Upstairs and downstairs on Aitchison, Topeka & Santa Fe's El Capitan service from Los Angeles to Chicago, 1956. The 'hotel on wheels' boasts dining penthouse style in the hi-level dining car, 'You enjoy soft music, magnificent views, and of course, tempting Fred Harvey dishes – all high above the noise of the kitchen below.' The Top of the Cap hi-level lounge car has, 'skylights in the roof, as well as wide picture windows. The staircase at center leads to the lower lounge. There is a refreshment bar and attendants on call.' Other staff on board included the El Capitan Courier Nurse for mothers with children and an Indian guide in full tribal costume whose commentary covered the scenery, history and legends of New Mexico.

FACING The downstairs lounge bar of Canadian Pacific's Scenic dome car, 1954 (LEFT) and upstairs on the City of San Francisco (RIGHT).

OVERLEAF Amtrak's California Zephyr stops at Grand Junction on its three-day transcontinental trip. The train runs from San Francisco (Emeryville) through Sacramento and Nevada to Salt Lake City and across the Rockies to Denver and finally through the plains of Nebraska to Chicago.

For the ultimate in 1970s' utilitarian interior design, experience Amtrak's California Zephyr (service number 6) from San Francisco (Emeryville) to Chicago. The 3-day trip crosses 2 time zones and travels at 72 km/h (45 mph) through the Rocky Mountains (ABOVE CENTRE) and at a top speed of 127 km/h (79 mph) through the night on the flat.

Accommodation choices are reclining coach seats, Superliner Standard bedrooms or – with private shower and toilet – Superliner Deluxe bedrooms (LEFT).

A Genesis diesel-electric locomotive built by General Electric Transportation Systems pulls a consist of 3 coach cars, 2 sleeper cars, a dining car and an observation car (FACING AND ABOVE) with café on the lower level.

Internal access from car to car is via the upper level only (ABOVE LEFT).

PARIS GOLDEN ARROW

Daily Pullman Service from London Victoria

Tickets and reservations from principal Travel Agencies or Continental Enquiry Office Victoria Station London SW1

TOP LEFT British Rail poster promotes the company's daily Pullman service between London and Paris, 1961.

TOP RIGHT Trianon Bar in the buffet car which operated on the prestigious Golden Arrow boat train between London's Victoria Station and Dover, 1946. The carriage was timber construction and built by Pullman Car Company in 1927.

ABOVE A rebuilt Bulleid Pacific locomotive, Merchant Navy class, sports a Golden Arrow headboard. Oliver Bulleid was the Chief Engineer on the Southern and introduced many innovative features in locomotive design.

FACING Royal Saloon, carriage No 9007 was built in 1945 for the Great Western Railway and was used by HM Queen Elizabeth, the Queen Mother.

sought to cover up the moving parts of the steam engine. Dreyfuss's belief in practical design, together with his early career as a theatre designer, gave the Pacifics an evolutionary look – he highlighted the six-driving-wheel configuration by arching the shroud to expose the huge 2 metre (79 inch) drivers and coupling rods. By painting a black circle on each wheel, the designer gave the impression of a white-wall tyre in negative, very fashionable for the age. Further theatre was achieved by illuminating the driving mechanism with concealed spotlights. The understated livery consisted of the NYCS logo on the nose and 'The Mercury' painted in aluminium, just below the cab windows.

At Dreyfuss's behest, NYCS's Beech Grove shops in Indianapolis gutted the seven redundant commuter cars to provide the blank canvas for the new buffet-lounge, diner, parlour and parlour-observation carriages. To create the impression of an single, articulated vehicle, the access openings between cars were widened, to create semi-circular vestibules. The theme of flowing continuity throughout was enhanced further by the consistency of the interior decor, the branded china and the clean, contemporary furnishing. The Mercury lived up to the publicity department's slogan, 'The Train of Tomorrow'.

With the success of the Mercury under his belt, Dreyfuss went on to design the jewel in NYCS's crown, the 20th Century Limited and, in doing so, created an exceptional train. He worked with Alco to style the Hudson locomotive, which would lead the new fleet on the company's famous Water Level Route between New York and Chicago. Dreyfuss's iconic solution was to exploit the natural shape of the locomotive and, again, as in the case of the Mercury, expose the driving mechanism. Design details included three steps that punctured either side of the pilot cowl and lead the eye (and the feet) up to the hemispherical nose, accented by a vertical fin that grew in proportion as it reached the air intakes on

ABOVE LEFT The Queen's dressing room and bath on the Royal train run by the London, Midland & Scottish, 1937.

LEFT Exterior handrail on King Edward VII's carriage and service bells mounted on the rosewood-panelled interior saloon walls. The carriage was built by the London & North Western Railway in 1902 and featured the first electric cigar lighter.

ABOVE The interior of Queen Adelaide's saloon arranged for sleeping, 1840. A cushion is laid between the seats; on the left is a flap which, when raised, opened up a connecting boot; this added some extra space beyond the confines of the carriage so that Adelaide could lie comfortably with her feet projecting into the boot. The saloon was built by the London and Birmingham Railway.

FACING ABOVE Prime Minister Winston Churchill insisted that the Royal train be armoured with steel plating at the outbreak of World War II. The wooden carriage had been built in 1941 for King George VI and the Queen Mother. The interior decoration, though comfortable, was not overly plush in order to reflect the austerity of the war years. The carriage was last used by Queen Elizabeth II in 1977.

FACING BELOW Deltic Class with Queen of Scots headboard.

top, at the front of the skyline casing. A single headlight, mounted slightly below centre of the prow, completed the effect – and the effect was a stunning success.

Inside and out, Dreyfuss used subtle tones of blue and grey, complemented with bare metals, to create a relaxed, metropolitan atmosphere on the 20th Century Limited. Pullman-Standard's 16-car consist provided a combination of roomettes, bedrooms (with hot showers), lounges and dining areas. Walls were covered in walnut or leather, and sofas upholstered in grey leather and chairs in tan pigskin graced the observation lounge. Lighting was dimmed after dinner, and music was piped in as the diner was transformed into a nightclub. The elite accommodation suited the chic clientele, and celebrity encounters were promised by Pullman-Standard's magazine advertising: 'A visit to the bar lounge of the *20th Century* is an experience akin to being a guest in a famous and exclusive club. For rarely does the *Century* move without a quorum of internationally known people aboard. And, as the social center of this magnificent train, it is here that you will encounter them.' The union of utility and understated design, with just a hint of futurism, produced what many consider the most handsome of all locomotives. A few critics likened Dreyfuss's 1938 Hudson to a streamlined kitchen appliance, but the passengers were undeterred and embraced the avant-garde.

Henry Dreyfuss was a true pioneer of industrial design. He illustrated his 'designing for people' philosophy by creating Joe and Josephine. The typical American couple were part of his development of anthropometrics – the classification of human dimensions – which were used in product prototyping. They have since become a key component of the industrial-design process.

From the 1930s to the 1950s, America dominated passenger-locomotive design, with inspired creativity under the expert eye of stylists like Kuhler and Dreyfuss, but also Walter Dorwin Teague,

ABOVE A liberal use of tartan for a British Rail 2nd-class carriage.

FACING Various British Rail mock-up and production interiors: Refurbishment proposals for Mk1 coaching stock in the late 60s and early 70s (1-3, 4 & 6); 1st-class compartment mock-ups for the XP64 ,the forerunner of the InterCity 125 (5 & 8); workstation concept for the APT, the padded armrests denote 1st class (7); passenger coach Mk 2a, 1982 (9); InterCity sleeper-car lounge (designed by Jenny Stevens) from the mid 1980s (10) – the loose furniture would not be allowed today for safety reasons; a Mk1 buffet car refurbishment from the 1960s (11); and a late 1970s buffet car with 'modern' fluorescent lights (12).

RIGHT The British Rail membrane seat allowed easy cover changing. The wooden prototype was used in ergonomic trials to ascertain optimum pitch and comfort. Tony Howard, who headed the British Rail design department, instigated production and development of a new seat, which then went into the Mk 3b Pullman's 1st class, and was to be the seat for the APT (Advanced Passenger Train). Both seats were the effective pioneers of the ergonomic shape which became standard for the next 15 years and upon which all future seat development was based. Innovative ergonomic work was also commissioned on the headrest area as part of the development; the unique feature of the 1st-class seat was its recline mechanism and geometry which actually brought the seat up to a dining position at the table, or relaxed it away from the table for lounge position. The original design concept was by Keith Wrightson.

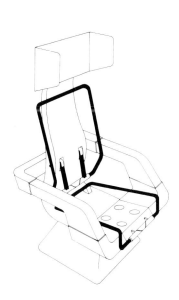

Norman Bel Geddes, Paul Cret, Brook Stevens and Raymond Loewy. Loewy emigrated from his native France in 1919, and, following a stint as a fashion illustrator, focused his attention on product design, restyling domestic and office goods. His first locomotive project was the cosmetic restyling of the electric GG-1 in 1934 for the Pennsylvania Railroad. By smoothing its riveted body through the process of arc-welding and by redesigning the livery, he established his reputation and gained other rail clients, such as Northern Pacific, Delaware & Hudson and the Baldwin Locomotive Works. More commissions followed, including the 1939 S-1, displayed at the New York World's Fair. The huge, sleek locomotive, renamed 'American Railroads' for the exhibition, ran on a treadmill, so that spectators could see the workings of the impressive 6-4-4-6 wheel configuration. The smooth contours were headed by the increasingly popular bullet-nose, with centrally mounted headlight.

Also on exhibition at the 1939 New York World's Fair was an eight-car train, led by the 'Duchess of Gloucester' engine. The Coronation-class Pacific was designed by Sir William Stanier, London Midland & Scottish Railway's Chief Mechanical Engineer, and showed that developments by the French, Germans and British were setting new levels of aerodynamics for the steam locomotive. The Coronation class, although not always in streamlined form, hauled many of the heaviest trains on Britain's West Coast route until the end of the steam age. Stanier's contemporary at the London & North Eastern Railway, Sir Nigel Gresley, was responsible for the design of the legendary Mallard. This A4-class locomotive attained the world record for the fastest steam engine in 1938 – a staggering 203 kilometres (126 miles) per hour.

Streamlining and speed trials inspired the public and served as useful publicity for the train companies. Yet steam was not the only method of propulsion in development at this time; as early as

ABOVE The commuter train is a demanding environment for the furniture and the industrial designer. Atlantic Design created the Grammer seat for South West Trains Desiro UK; the endoskeletal design offers more legroom for the passenger behind and the extraction of a cushion for repair is simplified by a couple of fixings under the leading edge. The cushion can be replaced with a spare that is integrated into the back of the seat.

FACING Sleepy-Hollow was the registered trade mark for 'the most comfortable seat possible'. The chair was designed in 1944 by Dr Hooten, Chairman of the Department of Anthropology at Harvard University. Over 3,000 people were measured as part of the development programme.

ERECTED OVER
L·N·E·R LINE—
MILNGAVIE STATION
(NEAR GLASGOW)

Swift
Safe
Sure

THE GEORGE BENNIE
RAILPLANE SYSTEM OF TRANSPORT

LEFT AND BELOW Scottish engineer George Bennie built a monorail railplane test track at Milngavie, West Dumbartonshire above an existing London & North Eastern Railway station. His idea was to have passengers travel by railplane and freight traffic to continue using land rails in an effort to speed up passenger services. Launched in 1930, the railplane was powered by large propellers at both ends, making it capable of 193 km/h (120 mph). Due to a lack of further financial backing Bennie's revolutionary monorail system progressed no further and was declared bankrupt 7 years later.

FACING The Transrapid 07 on the Emsland test track in 1990. On August 14, 1934, German engineer Hermann Kemper received a patent for the magnetic levitation of trains. In 1979, 8 years after the first passenger test, the magnetic levitation technique had its public debut. Renowned designer Alexander Neumeister took advantage of the fact that magnetic levitated trains were not bound by existing structures and allowed for more generous dimensions on the cross-section. By abolishing rows of seats Neumeister offered the passenger an hitherto unknown perspective – an unobstructed view through the front window. A design that he implemented in Die Bahn's high-speed ICE 3 20 years later.

In 2003, at 501 km/h (311 mph) the Shanghai Transrapid, China set up a new world record for commercial railway systems and a year later welcomed its one-millionth passenger on the world's first commercial Transrapid route.

FACING BELOW Swedish industrialist Dr Axel Lennart Wenner-Gren was the first to build a monorail test track after World War II. Seen here is the scaled-down train which attained speeds of almost 160 km/h (100 mph) on an oval test track in Fuhlingen, Germany in 1952.

1903, in conjunction with Allgemeine Elektrizitäts Gesellschaft (AEG), German industrialist Ernst Werner von Siemens and his partner Johan Halske demonstrated the first high-speed electric express. At the Zossen military railway, near Berlin, their electric railcar reached 210 kilometres (130 miles) per hour and launched the future of truly high-speed rail travel. The internal combustion engine was also tested; as a form of propulsion Franz Kruckenberg's Schienenzeppelin (Rail Zeppelin), designed to carry 50 passengers, was powered by a BMW aircraft engine. In 1931, the railcar was assisted to a record speed of 230 kilometres (143 miles) per hour by a large, wooden propeller, which was mounted at the rear. Other less successful speed trials included Fritz von Opel's Rak 3 in 1928, which cannot be categorized as high-capacity rail transport, as it was designed to carry only one person. The doomed rocket-powered vehicle exploded seconds after a record run of 254 kilometres (158 miles) per hour. It was the outbreak of the Second World War that was to interrupt the racing of trains across the European landscape – at least for a few years.

The streamlining of European steam was quite different from the bullet-nosed and bathtub-shrouded American streamliners, perhaps not only as a consequence of differing cultural tastes, but also due to the designers involved. In America, industrial designers, with much experience in styling all manner of goods for the consumer market, were applying their own commercial-design sense to transport. In Europe, and particularly in Britain, mechanical engineers, with grounding only in rail transport, were styling with less flamboyance and more consideration for the medium – the understated style of engineer-designer.

Otto Kuhler, for one, believed streamlining to be discontinuous with good, honest design. Expressing his opinions to the New York Railroad Club in 1935, he said, 'Streamline freak locomotives have been

ABOVE Rhaetische Bahn's Schneeschleudern operates after fresh, heavy snowfall on the Bernina route. Some of the most spectacular mountain scenery in Europe is viewed through the picture windows and skylights of the Panoramawagen on Rhaetische Bahn's Bernina Express and Heidi Express.

FACING A Canadian Pacific Domeliner passes through Leanchoil, British Columbia in December, 1972.

built lately the world over. Most of them are badly conceived in their outline and their shrouding and covering; in most of them the inherent beauty and the "personality" of the steam locomotive is lost.'

Locomotives driven by steam dominated the railways until the end of the Second World War. Even in the mid-1970s, it was estimated that over 25,000 steam engines were still in use throughout the world. However, the end of the 1940s marked the beginning of the end of steam as the mainstay of motive power. Widespread dieselization and electrification were to create new shapes and forms on the rail horizon. Many diesel-electrics styled in the 1940s through to the 1960s bowed towards the 'form follows function' precept and, although significantly more efficient than steam, were, in the main, uninspired in appearance. Among the exceptions were the E- and F-Series, built by Electro-Motive Division of General Motors in the late 1930s, the Trans-Europe Express of 1957 and the English Electric's 1961 Deltic, with its sad-eyed windscreen and characterful face.

In Britain, after the Second World War, there followed almost two decades of struggle to revive the railways, which led the Chairman of the British Railways Board, Dr Richard Beeching, to make some drastic changes to the rail network. The rising annual deficit of the nationalized British Railways was cause for much concern. Beeching revealed that over half the track mileage carried only 4 percent of passenger miles. In contrast, the rest of the system had earnings that covered route costs by more than six times. As a consequence of the 'Beeching Report' of 1963, 8,047 route kilometres (5,000 miles) and 2,000 stations were closed. However, at least one positive outcome was a term repeated throughout the document – InterCity.

The Blue Pullman was the InterCity of the 1960s and was very successful. The diesel-electrics were air-conditioned, and meals were served at every seat. High speed, passenger comfort and service were

FACING ABOVE The fastest passenger train in 1966. The Japanese passenger train, the Tokaido, was known for its world record-breaking speed in transporting commuters of up to 210 km/h (130 mph) – it took just over 3 hours to travel the 515 km (320 mile) line between Tokyo and Osaka.

Japan's Bullet Train was launched on the high-speed Shinkansen (literally meaning 'new main line') in 1964. It shaped the future for rail transportation around the world setting standards that a number of other countries have since followed.

A JR West Shinkansen Series 0, built in 1976 (ABOVE AND RIGHT), now rests at the National Rail Museum, York, UK. Shown here is the drivers' cab and the passenger coach.

FACING BELOW Unlucky for some: Row 13 on the JR West Shinkansen Series 0. To date the Shinkansen service has maintained a flawless record of no passenger fatalities or injuries due to accidents.

OVERLEAF 100N and 300N series Shinkansen bullet trains at the yard at Shinjuku Station, Tokyo, 1996. Shinjuku is one of the most frequented train stations in the world with more than 2 million passengers per day.

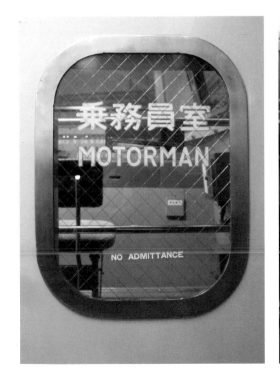

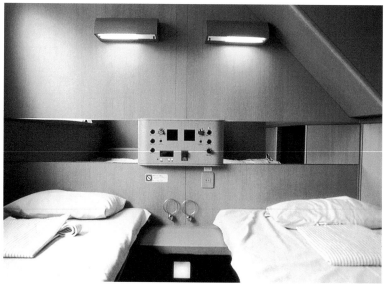

ABOVE Inaugurated in 1998, JR
West's sleeping-car service Sunrise
Express runs from Tokyo to
Shikoku and from Tokyo to Tottori.

FACING Regarded as the fastest
electric train in commercial
operation in 1998, a Nozomi 500
series Shinkansen rests at
Hiroshima Station, Japan.
   A synthesis of aerodynamics,
technology and design, the
Nozomi Shinkansen was designed
by Alexander Neumeister and
teams from JR West and Hitachi.

key to regaining a convincing share of the travel market from motorways and airlines. In 1968, inspired by results in France, Germany and Japan, British Railways appointed Terry Miller as Chief Engineer, to oversee the development of an Advanced Passenger Train (APT). The InterCity 125 high-speed diesel led the new service and was to rank as one of British Rail's greatest achievements. The public responded with enthusiasm to shorter journey times, greater comfort and improved on-board service. British Rail's InterCity became Europe's only profitable rail business and not only inspired the new operating companies following rail privatization in the 1990s, but was also imitated throughout the continent.

At the beginning of the 1960s, the ideas of high-speed travel based on magnetic levitation technology (Maglev), rather than conventional track, began to be mobilized in France. It was shelved, however, for practical and economic reasons. Gas-turbine trains, powered by the same engines as those used in helicopters, were considered by Société Nationale des Chemins de Fer Français (SNCF) in the late 1960s, until the oil crisis of 1974 prompted them to be displaced by the experimental electric railcar, Zébulon. In 1976, the first batch of production Train à Grande Vitesse (TGVs) were tested. After rectifying a number of stability problems, over 15,000 modifications, in fact, the TGV 100 got into the record books by reaching a top speed of 380 kilometres (236 miles) per hour. In September 1981, President Mittérand inaugurated the first public-service TGV, and so began the great tradition of French high-speed rail travel.

British ex-patriot Jack Cooper was the industrial designer of the original TGV, and had the necessary qualifications, having been an apprentice to Raymond Loewy. Cooper's skill was to address the sometimes contradictory design requirements regarding the interior design; the interiors had to be welcoming, relaxing and comfortable, but also easy to clean and maintain. His team at builders Alsthom

LEFT, ABOVE AND FACING In 1998, Virgin Trains announced its order for fifty-five 225 km/h (140 mph) eight-car electric trains, and seventy-eight 201 km/h (125 mph) four- and five-car diesel electric trains, representing a £2.25 billion investment to replace their existing fleet of West Coast Main Line and Cross-country vehicles. Priestman Goode, JHL and Start Design were appointed as the Virgin design team for the two new fleets of trains. The focus of the brief was to translate the Virgin brand identity into all aspects of the passenger experience, from the exterior nose to the interior, including seating, shops, galleys and on-board service.

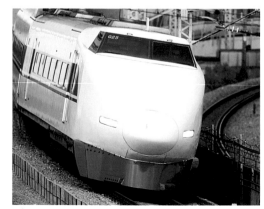

ABOVE The controls on the ICE 3 (Inter City Express) run by Die Bahn at Brussels-Midi awaiting departure for Cologne, March, 2004.

RIGHT Die Bahn's ICE 3. Passengers are able to share the driver's view of the track ahead through the large windscreen.

FACING ABOVE AND LEFT Driver's cab of the Mallard steam locomotive. The class A4 locomotive was designed and built by Sir Nigel Gresley at the London & North Eastern Railway's Doncaster Works in 1938. In July of the same year it reached a speed of 203 km/h (126 mph), achieving a new world record for steam locomotives. The interior of the cab shows the firebox, pressure gauges and boiler.

FACING RIGHT Driver's cabin and exterior of JR West's 100 Series.

THIS PAGE The Kyushu Railway Company's Series 800 Tsubame Express incorporates the latest technology with traditional craftsmanship perpetuated by the people of Kyushu; one such example is the rope curtains in the washrooms, crafted with *igusa* rush grown in Yatsushiro. The seats are upholstered over bent wooden frames and the partitions are made of camphor wood. Delicate wooden blinds provide shade from Kyushu's bright sunlight.

FACING On Kyushu Railway Company's 787 Ariake Express the semi-compartment (CENTRE) offers a degree of privacy.

designed everything from seats to door handles, and while the interior design went through a highly iterative process, the exterior was approved immediately.

As technology advances, the relationship of industrial designer and engineer becomes ever closer. Axle weight is a critical issue at high speed – the heavier the carriage, the higher the maintenance costs of track and train. Such materials as aluminium and composites help to keep weight down. Using computer analysis to achieve the least possible use of materials in construction and design can also help; seats redesigned for the TGV Duplex reduced the weight of each unit by 12 kilograms (26 pounds), which, in turn, reduced the weight of each car by 1,000 kilograms (2,200 pounds). The marble washstands and bulky mahogany furniture of the early wagons-lits have no place in the twenty-first-century carriage.

The reduction of noise is desirable for passenger comfort and trackside residents. A train's nose profile and the aerodynamic shrouding of its cars not only assist energy consumption, but also reduce emitted noise. There are different noses for different environments; the shape of Eurostar's nose, for instance, is optimized for its passage through the Channel Tunnel. One of the most attractive noses in the train industry belongs to German rail system Die Bahn's electric ICE 3, the styling of which was created by Alexander Neumeister. The third-generation ICE train entered service in 2000 and was designed for operations throughout Europe. Seat numbers 11 and 13 in the first and last cars have the best view of the track ahead through the sloping, oval window, and over the left shoulder of the driver to the instrument panel (if in the front carriage). A glass wall separates the driver from the passengers. The sleek, white Inter City Express glides on rails and very quickly reaches a cruising speed of 270 kilometres (170 miles) per hour. Its top speed is 300 kilometres (185 miles) per hour. Inside, at the end of

ABOVE The colourful interior of the centre booth and the well-appointed lavatory and washroom on JR Kyushu's 883 Sonic Express.

FACING The 883 Sonic Express motif is influenced by the distinctive flared 'ears' of the seat headrests and discreetly applied to the front of the train.

each carriage, a screen displays the arrival time at the next destination, as well as the current time, wagon number and current speed. The pressurized cars and smoothness of ride are reminiscent of air travel, and audio sockets in seats (and video screens in the backs of first-class seats) contribute to the aeronautical ambience. Walls are finished in jade green, translucent glass and wood veneer. There are fax machines and lap-top connections and, in the corridors, touch screens provide transit information and online booking. An enclosed family compartment, with play area for children, is situated next to the Bord Restaurant. In the same wagon, a kitchen services the snack bar. A semi-circular, counter-style guard's compartment is very approachable, giving the effect of a welcoming reception desk in a chic, metropolitan hotel. The future is tilting as Siemens are supplying Die Bahn with the ICE-T, a train that can handle curves at higher speeds and, as a result, will provide an even faster service.

The original inspiration for high speed in Europe was the incredibly successful Japanese National Railways' Shinkansen, commonly known as the Bullet Train, which began operations in 1964. Passenger traffic between Japan's main cities of Tokyo and Osaka had become congested, following the recovery of the economy after the Second World War. The Japanese government bravely committed to the building of a new 515 kilometre (320 mile) line, dedicated to passengers only. Topographic obstacles led to the construction of numerous tunnels, with 30 percent of the route elevated on viaducts and bridges. The new trains, capable of 250 kilometres (155 miles) per hour, halved travel times, and the enormous investment paid off as passenger traffic grew threefold over the next nine years.

The original 0-Series Shinkansen was put into service on completely new track, and an automated self-signalling system on the trains dispensed with the need for trackside signals. All relevant information was passed down the main conductor wires to the driver. Further innovations included

THIS PAGE AND FACING Die Bahn's high-speed ICE trains have been in use since 1991, providing a fast service between Germany's cities. The sleek trains operate with almost no engine noise and offer the comfort of pressurized carriages, so when passing through tunnels ear discomfort is eliminated. There are passenger cars along with restaurant and café stations on board. There are fax machines, phones, outlets for laptops and video screens.

Touch-screen information in the vestibules offers online booking facilities and train timetables.

OVERLEAF Leather abounds in first class on the ICE 3 en route to Köln, Germany, 2004.

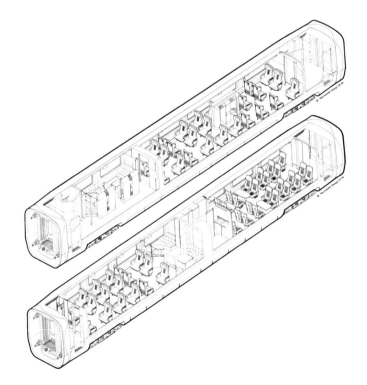

seismographs in the main control centres, which automatically stopped all trains if an earthquake threatened. Even by today's standards, the shape of the early 1960s' Shinkansens was distinctive. The 16-car train set looked as though it had evolved from the drawing board of an aircraft engineer.

The twenty-first-century Shinkansen fleet includes the 300-, 500- and 700-Series trains, each with a passenger capacity of 1,323. Carriages are wider and longer than their European counterparts, providing spacious accommodation. Seats can be rotated to face forwards or backwards, to suit direction preference or social predilection. Another important member of the Shinkansen fleet is the high-speed inspection train. Doctor Yellow, so called because of its sulphurous hue, inspects the electrical facilities every ten days, while travelling at speeds of up to 270 kilometres (170 miles) per hour. Meanwhile, the new N700-Series, which boasts improved passenger comfort and 'harmony with environment', utilizes an aerodynamic double-wing nose shape, which contributes to its maximum speed of 300 kilometres (185 miles) per hour.

Japanese National Railways was privatized in 1987, resulting in the three main operating companies that cover the country's west, east and central areas. Today, on the Tokaido Shinkansen (Tokyo to Osaka), JR Central services 355,000 passengers a day, runs 12 trains an hour during peak times from Tokyo station and averages an annual delay of just 24 seconds per train. Moreover, the Shinkansen service has maintained a flawless record of no passenger fatalities or injuries due to accidents throughout its 40-year history.

The future of rail transport is wheel-less, as research and development continues once again into magnetic levitation. Maglev offers significant advantages over existing technologies. With its contact-free support, high-speed propulsion and advanced braking systems, it is energy-efficient, thus better for

ABOVE La Chaise Haute Couture: in a fresh approach to the on-board experience for the 3rd generation of TGV for SNCF, the agency MBD Design worked in collaboration with fashion designer Christian Lacroix and railway seating manufacturer Compin to create a sophisticated and practical solution.

FACING Au Revoir: a parting kiss before boarding the late-running TGV at Brussels-Midi Station, Belgium, 2004.

the environment, and passenger-friendly. Since the Yamanashi Maglev Test Line in Japan opened in 1997, 50,000 test-ride passengers have been recorded over a total test-run distance of 300,000 kilometres (185,000 miles), at speeds exceeding 550 kilometres (340 miles) per hour. JR Central and the Japan Railway Construction Public Corporation are conducting topographical surveys in anticipation of a new 500 kilometre (310 mile) route between Tokyo and Osaka, with a predicted travel time of one hour.

Operational surveys and project development in Germany, the Netherlands and the USA have been carried out by Transrapid International, who were responsible for the world's first Maglev line, connecting Pudong Airport with Longyang Road Station in Shanghai, China. Since its maiden journey in 2002, thousands of passengers have glided along at speeds of 430 kilometres (270 miles) per hour, making it the fastest railway system in commercial operation.

In environmental terms, the electric train and the Maglev should be the future of all high-capacity passenger travel, but, of course, cost and travel time are always the deciding factors, and competition with the airlines continues. The energy required to carry one passenger 1 kilometre (1/2 a mile) in a commercial aircraft is four times that of a train. Passenger flights emit more than 8 million tons of carbon-dioxide gas every year, and the increase in air travel will eventually create unsustainable levels of noise and air pollution. CO_2 emissions from a Boeing 747 are ten times greater than that of a 700-Series Shinkansen.

Apart from a few exceptions, trains run only across countries and continents; a transatlantic or transpacific high-speed rail route seems improbable. However, a visit to the Science Museum in London to marvel at the early innovation of Robert Stephenson's Rocket fires the imagination to ponder the possibilities of high-capacity passenger transport over the next 200 years.

SERVICE

Cafés, dining cars and provisioning

Mild anticipation greets me when I order food on a train. In an attempt to avoid disappointment, I assume a positive attitude by bringing to mind a quotation from Christopher Isherwood's novel *Mr Norris Changes Trains*. Mr Norris, contemplating a hock from the wine list, advises a fellow passenger, 'On a train one must always be prepared for the worst.'

In the early years of rail travel in Britain, before the advent of on-board catering, the passenger either packed a picnic hamper or made use of the numerous station restaurants. Entrepreneurs were to recognize the rail passenger as a captive market, however, and began to supply prepared luncheon baskets. Principal stations offered a choice of hampers to suit individual pockets and, in one case, it seems, socio-political inclination – for 2 shillings and 6 pence, 'The Democratic' consisted of a pint bottle of ale, a couple of pieces of non-descript meat, or a meat pie, and bread and cheese. At twice the price, 'The Aristocratic' featured chicken, ham and tongue, cheese, bread, butter and a condiment, washed down with the choice of either a pint of claret or a half-pint of fortified wine.

Tastes have changed over the years. The Great Depression of the early 1930s in America, and, to a greater extent, the two World Wars, severely interrupted the growth of rail services on both sides of the Atlantic, which were either cut back to skeletal operations, commandeered for military use or, simply, ground to a halt. Particularly in Europe, recuperation was slow but, in time, economic stability returned, and post-war prosperity enabled a wider public to take to the rails. Life on board the train imitated street life; by the 1950s, rail catering companies had introduced disposable 'crockery'; and the paper plates and styrofoam cups of fast-food culture were here to stay. In Britain, trolleys that dispensed scaldingly hot tea and iced buns on the station platforms were slimmed down and adapted for use on board, selling prepackaged food, covered in 'cellophane', or plastic wrap.

PREVIOUS PAGES One of the numerous service platforms at Chicago's Union Station. 50,000 commuters pass through the station every day, about half of the number of the boom years of the 1940s.

TOP Bar service on the Union Pacific Railroad in the 1970s. The mural in the background depicts the historic completion of the American transcontinental railroad at Promontory, Utah in 1869 and subsequent locomotives run by the Union Pacific Railroad.

ABOVE Takeaway lunchbox from the Refreshment Department of the North Eastern Railway, UK.

FACING American tourists being served drinks on the Devon Belle, May 1953. This Southern Region train ran from Waterloo to Plymouth, in competition with the Great Western Railway trains from Paddington, but stopped its service at the end of the 1954 season.

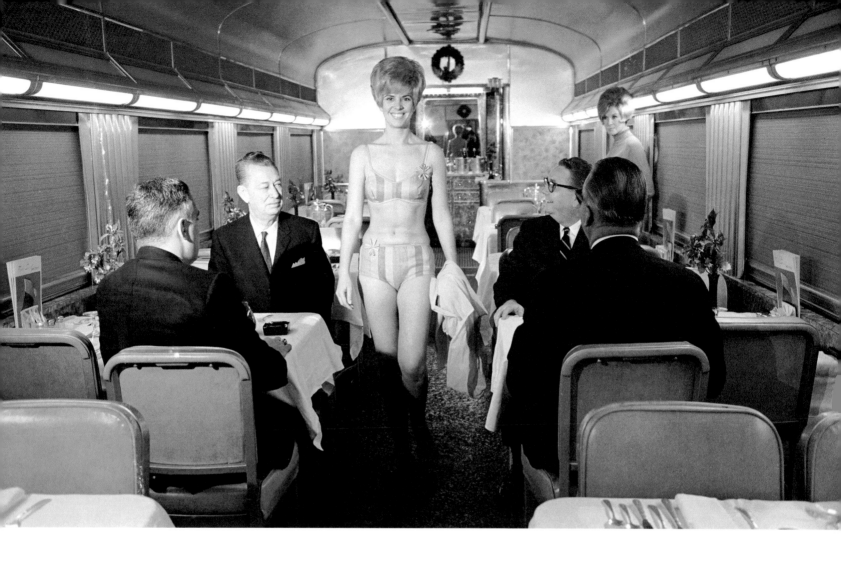

ABOVE Bikini-clad Carol Herring shows hospitality to passengers on the Seaboard Coast Line's 'Florida Special' train which ran between New York City and Florida. Besides hostesses in bathing suits, this super-deluxe train service provided guests with a recreation car for fashion shows, movies, television, live music and other diversions,1967.

FACING AND RIGHT The Zephyrettes began service in1949 and were the heart and soul of the California Zephyr. They were the primary point of contact for the passenger, and so became the ambassadors for the train. Western Pacific Railroad's company magazine outlined Zephyrette propriety, 'She must conduct herself with dignity and poise, and avoid any familiarities and acceptance of invitations from passengers or employees of the railroads. The Zephyrette is not permitted to drink or smoke while in uniform, and she must avoid spending time with passengers while they are drinking.'

ABOVE Meeting and greeting: a stewardess and a porter welcome passengers aboard, USA.

FACING ABOVE A conductor and engineer compare notes prior to departure on the Trans-Canada Limited, 1929.

FACING LEFT A railway porter stands on weighing scales at Marylebone Station, London, UK.

FACING RIGHT Southern Railway's Tea Service: tea ladies supply passengers at Waterloo Station with hot beverages and cakes served from a specially designed trolley. London, UK, 1946.

Once upon a time in the UK, there was no such thing as The British Rail Sandwich. A heartening thought perhaps, although statistics reveal that, despite its poor reputation, the 'Traveller's Fare' item was surprisingly popular. Tens of millions of sandwiches have been sold to meek rail travellers, who were resigned to the fact that, while satisfying their hunger, the snack did little to stimulate the palate. It was a sandwich of contradictions; it could be cold and soggy, or stale and hard, and the corners of the isosceles triangle-shaped bread would often curl up like the pages of a well-thumbed paperback. On display at the National Railway Museum in York, a document issued by the Director of British Rail Catering in 1971 gives precise instructions to food-preparation staff on how to make the sandwich. It was considered important that the consumer be able to see what lay between the two chalk-white slices of bread; at least a third of the filling had to be placed in the centre, where the diagonal cut would be made. Portion control dictated exact weights: 21 grams ($^3/_4$ ounce) of cheese and 7 grams ($^1/_4$ ounce) of gherkin, 19 grams ($^2/_3$ ounce) of luncheon meat and $^1/_{12}$ punnet of cress, 19 grams ($^2/_3$ ounce) of sardine and 9 grams ($^1/_3$ ounce) of the infamous cause of the overall sodden result – sliced tomato. The British Rail Sandwich served its purpose and still lurks in the chiller cabinets of mediocre catering franchises, albeit packaged under different brand names. What the sales statistics do not indicate is that its popularity was probably due to the meagre choice of rail food in Britain in the 1970s and 1980s.

Culinary globalization has contributed to the demand and supply of a more varied selection of food on trains and has given rise to some enticing multicultural hybrids. In the UK, Virgin Trains' Pendolino service currently offers an American-Chinese favourite, 'Chow Mein Noodles with Stir-Fry Vegetables', a Scottish-American 'Aberdeen Angus Cheeseburger', or a Lebanese-meets-New-York-deli composite of 'Grilled Asparagus and Chestnut Mushroom in Tomato Wrap'.

ABOVE A refreshment service trolley of the Great Western Railway dispenses alcoholic drinks, sandwiches, fruit and hot tea. Paddington Station, London, 1915.

RIGHT A guard on the London & North Western Railway signals to the driver by waving his flag and announces the departure of the train by blowing his whistle, 1922.

FACING Train conductors, 1910.

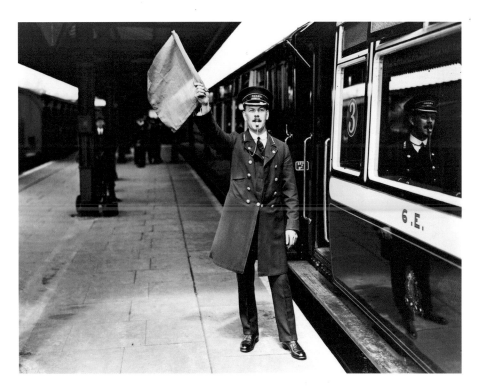

RIGHT Stewardesses attend the 787 Relay Tsubame Express – one of the trains run by the Kyushu Railway Company. Japan, 2003.

FACING ABOVE The British Rail logo adorns the hat of a Purserette, 1960s.

FACING RIGHT British Rail Purserettes modelling uniforms made with moulded fabrics negating the use of darts or seams, 1969.

FACING LEFT Concept designs for a Purserette's uniform and the interior of an APT (Advanced Passenger Train). UK, 1974.

FOR PASSENGERS

株式会社 ジェイアール東海パッセンジャーズ

The Victorians' attitude to eating in public was one of modesty, and most passengers preferred to retire to their own compartments to partake of their victuals. Initially, there had been a resistance to the concept of an on-board diner; the notion of an audience of the lower classes at the trackside or on the station platform witnessing the well-to-do relish a small banquet was considered vulgar. In addition, rail companies were loath to jeopardize the healthy patronage of the station restaurants and hotels under their management. It was only after the success of a multi-class diner, introduced by the Great Eastern Railway in 1891, that opinions began to change. The diner comprised three carriages, which serviced the boat-train on the York-to-Harwich route. The oil-fired kitchen was situated in the middle car, with first- and second-class sections each seating 18 passengers. The other two cars accommodated second- and third-class passengers in coach seats, the latter providing the country's first third-class dining compartment.

Victorian Britons were latecomers to the diner; on the other side of the Atlantic 24 years earlier, the Great Western Railway of Canada had employed railcar builder George Mortimer Pullman to design and produce the President. This hotel car provided sleeping quarters and a restaurant that served simple, but nourishing, fare – a plate of steak and potatoes for 60 cents or ham for 40 cents. In 1868, Pullman built the first full-length diner for the Chicago, Alton & St Louis Railroad. He named it 'Delmonico' after the famous New York restaurant, and its success prompted Pullman to move further into food service, which precipitated the widespread adoption of on-board catering operations by many other railroads. Despite the comparative comfort and luxury of the North American railcars of the late nineteenth century, the distance and duration made the rail journey both arduous and monotonous. The introduction of the dining car added a fresh perspective to the rail passenger's

FACING ABOVE The shape of the new. The Nozomi 500 Shinkansen was regarded as the fastest train in commercial operation until the Series 700 succeeded in 1999. Crew change at Shin-Osaka Station, 1998.

FACING AND RIGHT The Central Japan Railway Company (JR Central) offers the 'For Passengers' service on all major high-speed routes. The pursers may individualize their uniforms with a choice of four different-coloured silk scarves. In the guise of the train hostess they also have a choice of overall garment with cherry-leaf pattern.

OVERLEAF Porters attend to passengers' luggage on Illinois Central Railroad's City of Miami. The cars, built by Pullman-Standard in 1940, bear the brown and orange paint scheme on Illinois Central's Chicago to Miami route. Fort Lauderdale, Florida 1956.

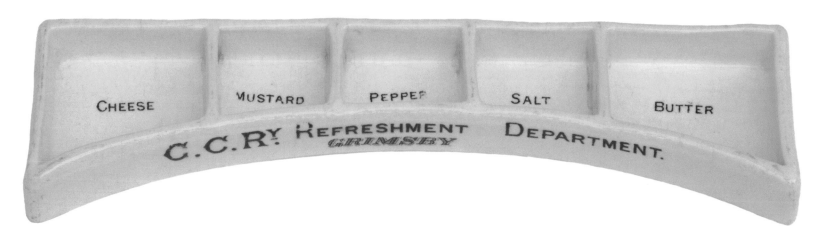

TOP Table service on the Trans-Canada Limited, 1924.

ABOVE Ceramic condiment tray provided by the Refreshment Department of the Great Central Railway. Made by W.T. Copeland of Stoke-on-Trent, UK, 1920.

FACING ABOVE Kitchen staff, stewards and passengers pose in the Hollyrood dining car on the Canadian Pacific Railroad, 1890.

FACING BELOW 'Dinner is served.' A steward chimes the call to passengers on a miniature xylophone. Trans-Canada Limited, 1920s.

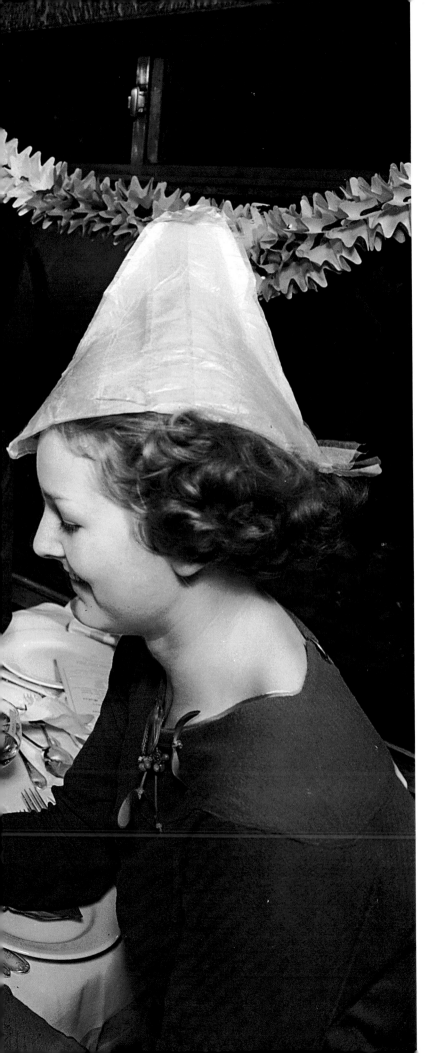

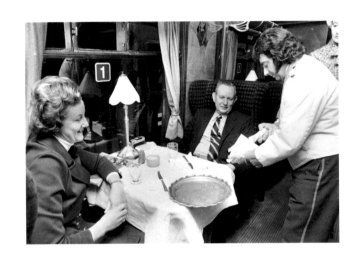

The
Lancastrian
Grill
Wine List

ABOVE A sommelier attends first-class passengers on the Brighton Belle Railway. UK, early 1970s.

LEFT A wine list dating from the 1960s as used on the buffet cars on the London-Manchester service named 'The Lancastrian' which operated under this title from 1957-1966.

FACING Festive fare: passengers enjoy Christmas dinner on a London Midland & Scottish train, 1950s.

royal carriages. Nagelmackers had commercially conquered western Europe and a little of eastern Europe; at the end of the nineteenth century, the Wagons-Lits company had 550 cars, carrying in excess of 2 million passengers per year, covering over 145,000 kilometres (90,000 miles) of railway line daily.

Today, Wagons-Lits continues to offer a luxury service in the form of the Orient Express, but there are now, of course, other ways of getting to Rome and other principal European destinations by train. Although not providing such opulent splendour, the twenty-first-century high-speed alternatives nevertheless guarantee a substantial degree of comfort, and most trains have cafés and a full restaurant service. In Spain, the Avé runs from Madrid to Seville, and so confident are the Spanish in the reliability of the service that they will refund your ticket if the train is more than five minutes late. The Italians run the Palatino sleeper from Paris to Rome, the tilting Cisalpino winds across the Alps from Lausanne to Milan, and on to Venice, and Eurostar Italia will speed you 320 kilometres (200 miles) from Florence to Rome in 90 minutes. Fast-food, quick-chill and microwave technology matches high-speed-train engineering – on many routes, the catering staff perform several different duties, working as chefs, waiting and bar staff. Eurostar, TGV, Thalys and Scandinavia's X2000 cover northern and western Europe, and Germany's Inter City Express (ICE), probably the best-appointed and most spacious of the European high-speed services, also travels east to Warsaw and Krakow. The food served on board Die Bahn's ICE train is pan-European and as healthy as you require. Breakfast choices include 'Fitness Frühstück', comprising fresh-fruit salad, croissant and orange juice, and monthly variations and specialties, devised in collaboration with specially invited 'guest' chefs, complement the hot-meal menu.

ABOVE A dining room with a view: a domeliner restaurant on board the Union Pacific Railroad, 1950s.

LEFT An illustration promoting Aitchison, Topeka & Santa Fe Railroad's El Capitan service, which was outfitted with double-deck cars from the Budd Corporation.

FACING ABOVE Haute Cuisine: a waiter serves a meal to first-class passengers on a SNCF train. France,1991.

FACING BELOW British Rail poster showing the full range of meals and snacks offered by the Travellers Fare service on Inter-City trains. UK, 1977.

BELOW The Mimbreno china was designed by architect Mary Colter for Aitchison, Topeka & Santa Fe Railroad's Super Chief routes. Her influence was motifs painted during the thirteenth century by the Mimbreno Indians of southwestern New Mexico. The original pottery was produced by Syracuse Pottery and was used by Santa Fe from 1937 until it ended passenger service in 1971.

21st-century high-speed service, on the ICE 3 (Inter City Express) en route to Berlin run by Die Bahn (ABOVE,) and on Eurostar (RIGHT) from London to Paris, 2004. Both the ICE and Eurostar trains also offer full restaurant service.

FACING British Railways buffet carriage, 1951. In addition to the counter service, stewards take passengers' orders for refreshments.

CAUTION: GAP BETWEEN CAR & PLATFORM

EXIT

EXIT

ABOVE AND LEFT Filling up at Grand Junction, Colorado. The kitchen is situated on the ground level of the double-decker dining car on Amtrak's *California Zephyr*. The water tanks hold 1137 l (250 gallons).

FACING Amtrak train in the process of being cleaned at Chicago's Union Station, Illinois, USA.

ABOVE LEFT Rise and shine: Amtrak Superliner Deluxe Bedroom with attendant. USA, 2001.

ABOVE Great Western Railway camping coach, 1936. Redundant railway carriages converted to provide holiday accommodation were introduced in 1933. The relatively low rent of about £3 ($5) a week made them popular and by 1935 there were over 200 located at various holiday destinations across the UK.

LEFT Great Western Railways breakfast china, 1938. Supplied by Ashworth Brothers of North Staffordshire, UK.

FACING ABOVE LEFT Inter-City Sleeper tray and Dudson Duraline crockery, 1986. Dudson Limited of Staffordshire has supplied railways in the UK and abroad since the beginning of the 20th century and continues to do so.

FACING ABOVE RIGHT British Rail poster promotes the Inter-City Sleeper service, 1980.

FACING RIGHT Southern Railways cube teapot, 1930s. The spout is discreetly located just below the top of the left-hand corner.

Eating habits vary greatly from country to country, often influenced by the style of the journey. In Japan, the Shinkansen high-speed train has cut journey times to such an extent that there is little demand for full restaurant service. There are buffets on board, but most passengers opt for the Bento box. This prepackaged lunch box usually contains a fish-and-rice dish with pickles, and is served by demure hostesses, who regularly proceed through the carriages with trolleys. Consumption statistics show loyal patronage and content passengers; on average, over 300,000 cups of tea are sold in one month on the 8,000 trains that run to and from Tokyo and Osaka, but coffee is the outright winner for beverage sales, totalling over half a million cups. (Coffee is also the West's favourite on-board drink.) On the same route, beer outsells sake and whiskey tenfold, and ice cream almost matches sales of the Bento-box favourite.

India's vast economic spectrum can be illustrated by the sustenance provided on its trains. Home-made picnics of rice wrapped in palm leaf are popular, and track-side vendors sell food items through the train windows from trays deftly balanced on their heads. Platform kitchen-buffets and kiosks sate the appetites of the majority of rail travellers. Regional expectations vary; at Virudhunagar Junction, in the southern state of Tamil Nadu, a breakfast of 'idli' (steamed rice cakes), accompanied by hot, sweet, milky 'chai' at the station buffet and a takeaway of 'vadai' (small, savoury lentil doughnuts) will set you up for the arduously slow, but spectacular, journey across the Western Ghats to Kollam, on the west coast. A restaurant car is provided on the long-distance, overnight Rajdhani Express, which services all major cities. At the affluent end of the scale, the 'Palace on Wheels' carries the wealthy tourist in extravagant luxury on a seven-night tour from Delhi to Agra. Once the domain of the ruling maharajas, the opulently furnished coaches consist of a series of restaurants, a library, a bar, several

IF
YOU HAVE TO
TAKE A
**LONG TRAIN
JOURNEY**
TAKE
YOUR FOOD
WITH YOU

BRITISH RAILWAYS
GWR · LMS · LNER · SR

ABOVE Evacuated from Dunkirk, Belgian soldiers wait to board a London-bound train at Margate on the Kent coast. UK, June 1940.

LEFT The four main British railway companies played a significant role in the evacuation of children from major cities in the summer of 1940 as fears of escalating aerial bombardment grew. The Great Western Railway ran 96 special trains, conveying nearly 70,000 children from London to the countryside. Maidenhead Station, Berkshire, June 1940.

FAR LEFT Poster produced for the Great Western Railway, London Midland & Scottish Railway, London & North Eastern and Southern Railway for display during World War II.

FACING Schoolboys from St. Bede's Prep School, Eastbourne, UK share treats from a tuck box, 1947.

ABOVE Food car on the Saigon to Hanoi Train, Vietnam.

RIGHT Snack on the Acela Express route. The Amtrak high-speed service on the east coast connects Boston and Washington via New York and Philadelphia.

FAR RIGHT Bento box lunch on board the Japanese Railway Kyushu train.

FACING ABOVE The healthy option: puri and fresh fruit available for passengers at Agra Cantonment station. Uttar Pradesh, India, 1995.

FACING LEFT A group of Japanese students enjoy box lunches washed down with cartons of Carnation milk on board Southern Pacific Lines, 1950s.

FACING RIGHT The Central Japan Railway Company (JR Central) offers the 'For Passengers' service on all major high-speed routes. The train hostess offers sushi, Bento box and other snacks from the trolley.

lounges and individually designed compartments, with en-suite bathrooms. As the name of the train suggests, service is of a royal standard, with a high staff-to-passenger ratio, including personal attendants. Restricted access and a policy of minimum disturbance to passengers require that tea trays are passed from carriage to carriage, by the waiters, on the outside of the train, very occasionally resulting in the loss of china, cutlery and condiments, but, as yet, not of staff.

Throughout today's world, on-board service and food reflect customers' expectations and attitude. As speed continues to be the obsession in the technological advance of rail travel and, as a consequence, a passenger-winning factor, so the grazing culture of our consumer-driven planet keeps pace. The long-distance Amtrak passenger can still partake of above-average fare in the sit-down restaurant car of the California Zephyr, albeit only for the duration of the actual consumption of the meal. Gone are the days of donning jacket and tie, and shooting the breeze over cocktails, before partaking of a three-course dinner in the high-level, glass-roofed Sky View café on Union Pacific's 'City of Los Angeles' domeliner.

The gastronomic delights of luxury train journeys aside, on-board food, although a secondary consideration to personal comfort and arriving on time, is an increasingly important cog in the marketing machine. Good eating, drinking and service encourage the passenger to return, and, when managed with creativity and expedience, provide tidy gains for the caterer and the rail company. Understandably, provision and profit at every opportunity is the underlying philosophy, and shifting units (preferably popular global brands) in high volumes and at high speed is the solution. The trend, it seems, is towards standing room only or high-stool-at-the-bar seating, in order to promote a policy of 'Eat up, drink up, pay up and make way for the next customer, please.'

The waiting game: a passenger contemplates as she awaits the departure of the local S-Bahn service from Friedrichstrasse Bahnhof, Berlin (FACING ABOVE). Catching 40 winks in the Great Hall of Chicago's Union Station, where the cavernous waiting room has 34 m (112 ft) high ceilings, marble floors and walls and Corinthian columns and was completed in 1925 (FACING BELOW). Awaiting the imminent arrival of the 9.55am high speed international ICE 952 train at Berlin's Zoologischer Bahnhof (RIGHT), 2004.

 Amtrak Cali

JACKING PAD

IDENTITY

Branding, livery and promotion

Fire-engine red, forest green and polished brass made up the liveries of the early steam age. A signwriter's classic drop shadow, cast from a deftly rendered number on the buffer plate, identified the locomotive. Names like 'Lion', 'Hercules' and 'Ajax' conveyed strength and speed. The physical characteristics of the engines determined the visual identity of the train, while coach lines in yellow and gold highlighted cab sides and wheel arches. Heraldry and coats of arms were the European equivalent of corporate branding in the nineteenth century, while in America company names, in the form of serif initial capitals, punctuated with ampersands, encouraged the public to guess the unabbreviated railroad title; St. P. & P. R. R. (St Paul & Pacific Railroad), B. & L. E. (Bessemer & Lake Erie) and C. & E. I. (Chicago & Eastern Illinois) were among a growing number of railroads to prosper in the industrious climate of the 'Golden Age' of steam.

Railroads of the nineteenth century relied on lithographic printers and signwriters to attract the attention of potential passengers. Typographers using block serifs and hot metal setting laid-out pamphlets and advertisements according to the Barnum-and-Bailey 'roll up, roll up' visual language of the day. With squirrel-hair brushes and mahl sticks, signwriters applied bespoke titles to every engine and coach. Gloss paint had not yet been invented; the base colour was matte, with several coats of varnish providing the gloss effect. In naming their engines, railroad companies sought individuality, in order to differentiate themselves from their competitors. In Europe, the naming of locomotives after royalty and nobility was popular. The Societa' Ferroviaria dell'Alta Italia (SFAI) began one of the first mountain railways in Europe in 1884, and named their locomotive after King Victor Emmanuel, who had been responsible for ending the Austrian occupation of northern Italy. In 1862, The London & North Eastern Railway began the operation of several, oddly named Problem-class engines, with

FACING The English Electric diesel-electric Deltic prototype, 1955, was extensively tested on the British rail network.

The Deltic is not only distinctive because of its powder-blue livery and chevron decoration but also for the single headlamp housing mounted on the front nose. Although never used to house a light whilst in use on British rail tracks, it was fitted for an unsuccessful attempt to export the engine to Canada.

ABOVE Great Northern Railway's Stirling No1 was designed by Patrick Stirling and built at Doncaster in 1870. The signature green and classic drop shadow is so indicative of Victorian train livery.

PREVIOUS PAGES Night stop at Sacramento, California, 2004. Amtrak's coach trailer 8025 is named Mokelumne River and dining car 8802 is named Sacramento Valley. The cars bear the multiple arrows logo used by Amtrak West business unit.

TOP The polished nameplate of the North Eastern Railway's 2-2-4 WT No 66 Aerolite built in 1869. The original Aerolite was a 2-2-2 built in 1851 by Kitson for the Great Exhibition and, in 1854, it entered the ownership of the North Eastern Railway (NER) who used it to haul the Mechanical Engineer's saloon coach; sadly it was destroyed in a collision in 1868.

ABOVE Great Western Railway branding attempts to dissuade the tempted pilferer at Paddington Station.

RIGHT 3rd-class livery of the East Coast Joint Stock; a common pool of passenger vehicles was operated by the Great Northern Railway, North Eastern and North British Railways. The main express trains departed from Kings Cross and Edinburgh Waverley and began running in June 1862. By the 1870s they were known as the Flying Scotsman.

FACING ABOVE The florid nameplate of the restored Southern Railways Bulleid Light Pacific, Blackmoor Vale, at Sheffield Park on the Bluebell Railway, UK.

FACING RIGHT The logos of 2 of the British 'big four': London & North Eastern Railway and the Great Western Railway.

diverse female designations, drawn from royalty, Greek mythology and more prosaic sources – 'Princess Royal', 'Atalanta' and 'Edith'. The French were practical when it came to christening their machines, more often than not using numbers, rather than words, although nicknames were a little more creative. The Paris, Lyon and Mediterranean Railway ran the Côte d'Azur Rapide express; high speeds were attributed, in part, to the casing between the chimney and the dome, the design of which reduced drag. The train became known as the 'coupe-vent', or 'windcutter'.

Understandably, there was limited scope for applying branding to steam engines. The name and/or number could only be painted on the front of the smoke-box door, on the arch of the splasher and on the cab and tender sides. Even if the equivalent of today's dedicated brand-strategy consultancy had practised in the late nineteenth century, the irregular outline of the steam locomotive and its multi-faceted form would still make it a challenge to apply a consistent and uniform identity.

The first suggestions of streamlining coincided with the gleaming train architecture of a new century. Art Deco's philosophy of unadornment and the aesthetics of other design movements led to an appreciation of raw materials. To their credit, the designers and manufacturers of the stainless-steel Zephyr for the Chicago, Burlington & Quincy Railroad in 1934 resisted the urge to cover the lustrous, three-car consist in paint. Architects Paul Cret and Holabird & Root understood that the shotwelded sheets of stainless steel defined the aerodynamic characteristics of this pioneering diesel-electric train; the train *was* the identity, and the discreet placement of a registration plate-style 'Burlington Route' logotype on its shovel-nose front and 'Burlington' on the leading-car sides was the only branding that it required. Once again, ancient mythology was the source for the name, with a number of variations, such as Zephyrus and God of the West Wind, being used in pamphlets and press advertising.

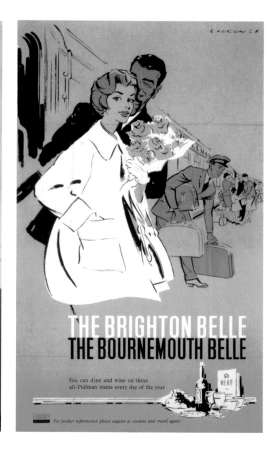

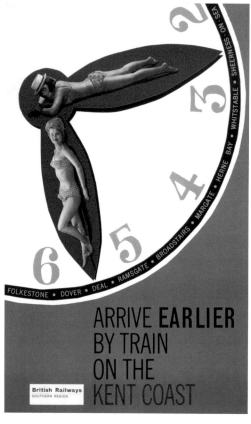

Sun, sea and British Railway advertising posters (clockwise from top left): 1975, 1961, 1960, 1961 and 1963.

FACING 1940 poster – 'It's quicker by rail' – the inter-war years saw a rise in the standard of living and the rise of the holiday camp. The railways played a large part in transporting holidaymakers around the country. Many took advantage of the 'send your luggage ahead' service available on most routes. Butlin's at Clacton-on-Sea opened in 1938 and closed at the end of the summer season in 1983.

BUTLIN'S HOLIDAY CAMP CLACTON-ON-SEA
IT'S QUICKER BY RAIL
ILLUSTRATED BOOKLET FREE FROM R. P. BUTLIN'S PUBLICITY DEPARTMENT. SKEGNESS. OR ANY L·N·E·R OFFICE OR AGENCY

Copywriters wrote lyrically of the 'Heritage from The Gods.... Glorified in stainless steel are the power and wisdom of Jupiter, the metallurgy of Vulcan, the beauty of Venus, the handicraft of Minerva, the legendary virtues of a dozen deities, plus the supernal, silent speed of Pegasus and Zephyrus.'

Romantic allegory and legend is a recurring theme in the rail company's quest to assign a personality to their engines. In England, the Queen Guinevere, weighing in at 141 tons, began service from the Southern Railway works at Eastleigh, Hampshire, as part of the King Arthur class in 1925. Other steam locomotives named by Southern Railway's public-relations department as part of the Arthurian-legend line-up included the king himself, as well as Sir Lancelot, Excalibur and Camelot. Mankind's inclination to humanize technology by imbuing it with symbolism may come from a basic desire to anthropomorphize the machine. From a marketing perspective, it is a tried and tested solution to suggest a relation between the might of engineered horsepower and the superhuman strength and endurance of a divinity.

In 1944, heavenly bodies collided with futurism to provide inspiration for General Motors' 'Train of Tomorrow'. While riding in the drivers' cab of a brand-new Electro-Motive diesel through Glenwood Canyon, Colorado, General Motors Vice President, Cyrus Osborn, witnessed the magnificent views first-hand and was convinced that passengers would be enchanted by the same experience – and so the domeliner was born. Pulled by the Electro-Motive Division's new E-7 passenger diesel, each of the four cars of the 'Train of Tomorrow' featured a double-glazed dome on the upper deck; they were named Star Dust, Sky View, Dream Cloud and Moon Glow. The livery continued the astral theme, with a wide belt of stainless steel wrapping the midriff of the predominantly dark-blue train; this was accented on the power car by the General Motors logotype, set in a graphic representation of a shooting star.

The rise and fall (and mergers) of the American railroads (LEFT TO RIGHT FROM TOP LEFT):

The use of the Yin and Yang symbol for the Northern Pacific Railway was suggested by Chief Engineer, Edwin Harrison McHenry following a chance sighting of the Korean flag at the Columbian Exposition in Chicago in 1893. The transcontinental Northern Pacific, created in 1864 merged into the Burlington Northern Railroad in 1970.

The Chicago, Rock Island and Pacific Railroad Company, commonly called the Rock Island, had its origins in 1847 and eventually served 14 states with nearly 8,000 miles of track. The line ceased operations in 1980.

Western Pacific's Scenic Limited ran a service from San Francisco to Chicago, also known as the Feather River Route, 1935.

Chicago, Milwaukee, St. Paul and Pacific Railroad Company (Milwaukee Road) operated in central and northern states. It began in 1863 and was merged into the Soo Line in 1986.

'Follow the Flag' was Wabash's by-line; also shown OPPOSITE heading the striking livery on an Electro-Motive diesel of 1946.

The New York Central System consisted of more than 10,000 miles of track by the end of the 19th century.

The Milwaukee Road's celebrated streamliners bore the name of the fourteenth-century chief of the Mohawks, Hiawatha.

Union Pacific Railroad's patriotic identity.

Pennsylvania Railroad's interlocking letters.

The Pan-American – Louisville & Nashville Railroad's pride on the Cincinnati to New Orleans overnight run, 1920s.

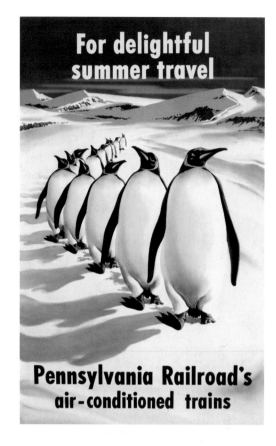

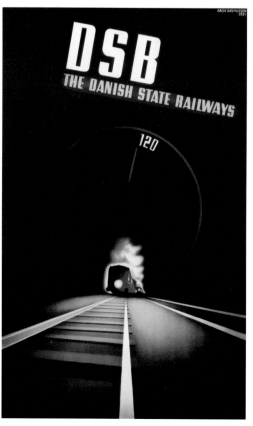

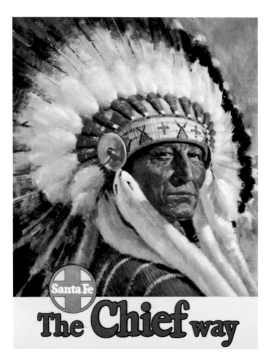

ABOVE Advertising posters (from left to right): 1951 by Dehaan, 1910 by David Dellepiane and 1936 (artist unknown).

RIGHT Aitchison, Topeka & Santa Fe's 'El Capitan: All-Chair-Car Transcontinental Streamliner via the Route of the Super Chief and The Chief', 1956.

FACING Advertising posters (clockwise from top left): 1952, 1950 (artists unknown), British Railways (Southern Region) reminds passengers to conserve warmth and fuel 1980s, 1930 by W.S. Bylityllis, 1937 by Aage Rasmussen, 1935 by Gert Sellheim.

FUNDY PARK

Seaboard Air Line was another railroad to embrace galactic branding, with its Silver Star, Silver Comet and Silver Meteor. General Motors' 1955 futurist Aerotrain was designed by Harley Earl, who was responsible for Oldsmobile and Corvette cars. The cost and performance of the Aerotrain were determined by a desire to make passenger business profitable for railroads. The epitome of 1950s' futurism, only three of these trains were ever built.

The tradition of train nomination based on legend and star systems has endured. In 1992, the Paris office of international branding consultants Design Strategy (now known as Minale Design Strategy) was in the initial stages of naming a new, high-speed European rail service. They were considering names based on Greek mythology – Greece being the birthplace of European civilization – in a reference to the greater European union that the proposed rail links between London and other capitals hoped to achieve. The brief from the collaborating French, British and Belgian partners was to find a name that people from all three of their countries could pronounce and understand. The solution: Eurostar, its identity formed from the tradition of rail 'stars' from the 1920s and 1930s – Northern Star, Blue Star and Star Express. Design Strategy wanted to get away from the practical, yet rather dry, approach used in the naming of other train services in the high-speed class, such as France's TGV, Britain's High Speed Train and Germany's ICE. The blue and yellow of the logotype reflect the colours of the European Union flag, although in slightly different tones. Design Strategy endeavoured to communicate a feeling of comfort and quality with the star and the soft, flowing lines of the identity. Interestingly, the yellow face of the distinctive wedge front, although not out of place, was not an element chosen by the design consultancy but, rather, was imposed by British legislation for safety reasons (despite the argument that if an errant member of the public sees yellow on a high-speed train

that is hurtling towards them, it is already too late). Minale Design Strategy went on to win a gold award in a French design competition for the Eurostar branding. The predominantly white livery and yellow-skirted sides still turn heads, even after more than a decade of service, and the unintentional, though visually pleasing, placement of the logotype's star just below the driver's side window hints at the hero status many schoolboys dream of achieving.

Eurostar has revolutionized travel between London, the south-east of England and northern Europe. By 2007, when new, high-speed track has been laid in the UK to match that on the continent, the travel time from the centre of London to the centre of Paris will be 2 hours and 15 minutes. Speed, convenience and reliability have contributed to the patronage of more than 7 million passengers annually since 1994, giving Eurostar the market lead on the London-to-Paris and London-to-Brussels routes, ahead of all airlines. The slick service and reputation of the brand has rekindled a cosmopolitan and aspirational attitude to rail travel for both the business and leisure markets. Eurostar is an aesthetically inspiring experience, as well as an inspiring train journey, from the train itself and the dedicated station architecture at Waterloo in London and at the Gare du Nord in Paris, to the award-winning 'non-uniform' staff uniforms, designed by Jacqueline de Baer. The inclusion of such celebrities as John Malkovich and Kylie Minogue in Eurostar's advertising and promotion, and Philippe Starck's smart and obliquely innovative refurbishment of station lounges and on-board interiors, continues to portray rail travel – at least in Eurostar's case – as chic and fashionable.

Creating an identity for a high-profile transport service has always transgressed simple aesthetics and ergonomics, using market research, psychology and a certain degree of philosophy in order to achieve the ultimate creative solution. It is not a new science; Henry Dreyfuss's holistic approach to the

Rail alphabet
Combined sheet - lowercase

	sheet no.	**1/12/1**
	issued	**Apr 1985**

This sheet must be used for all lettering applications in preference to sheets 1/11 and 1/12

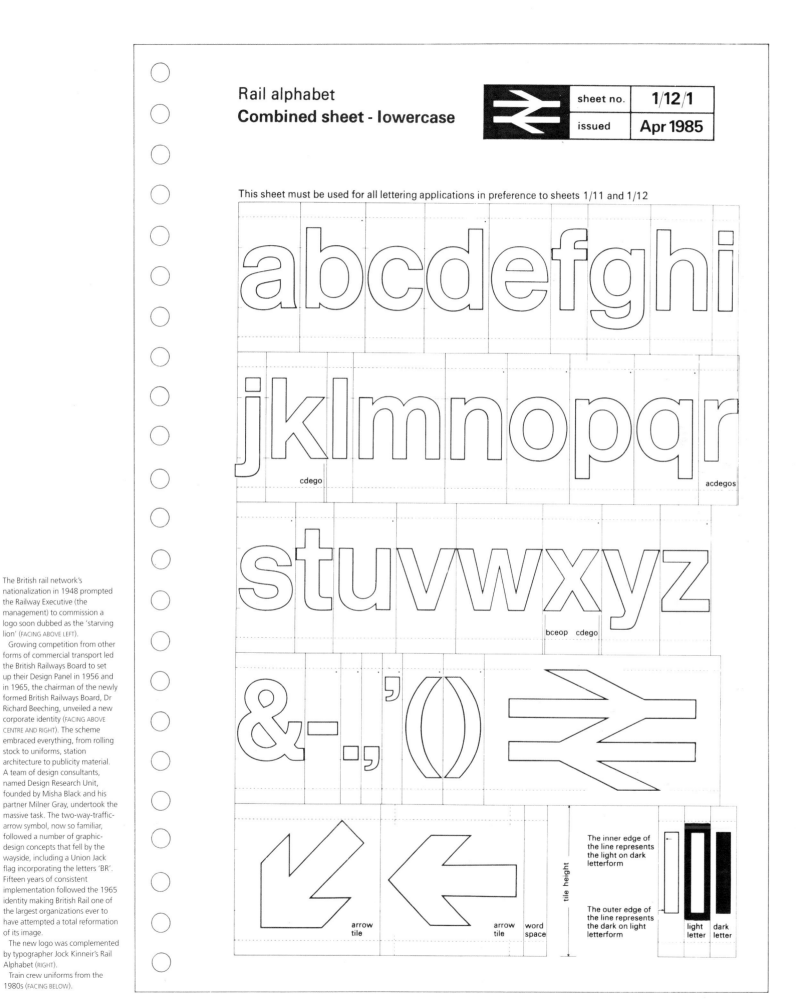

The British rail network's nationalization in 1948 prompted the Railway Executive (the management) to commission a logo soon dubbed as the 'starving lion' (FACING ABOVE LEFT).

Growing competition from other forms of commercial transport led the British Railways Board to set up their Design Panel in 1956 and in 1965, the chairman of the newly formed British Railways Board, Dr Richard Beeching, unveiled a new corporate identity (FACING ABOVE CENTRE AND RIGHT). The scheme embraced everything, from rolling stock to uniforms, station architecture to publicity material. A team of design consultants, named Design Research Unit, founded by Misha Black and his partner Milner Gray, undertook the massive task. The two-way-traffic-arrow symbol, now so familiar, followed a number of graphic-design concepts that fell by the wayside, including a Union Jack flag incorporating the letters 'BR'. Fifteen years of consistent implementation followed the 1965 identity making British Rail one of the largest organizations ever to have attempted a total reformation of its image.

The new logo was complemented by typographer Jock Kinneir's Rail Alphabet (RIGHT).

Train crew uniforms from the 1980s (FACING BELOW).

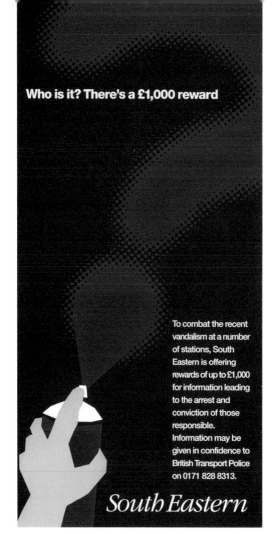

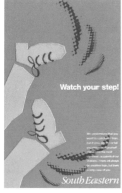

Who is it? There's a £1,000 reward

To combat the recent vandalism at a number of stations, South Eastern is offering rewards of up to £1,000 for information leading to the arrest and conviction of those responsible. Information may be given in confidence to British Transport Police on 0171 828 8313.

South Eastern

Mind the doors!

Watch your step!

South Eastern

South Eastern

Watch out!

Don't step on the tracks!

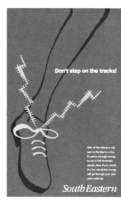

South Eastern

South Eastern

RIGHT Information and safety posters for the South Eastern railway, UK, designed by Johnson Banks in 1996 and illustrated by Michael Johnson, Harriet Devoy and Luke Gifford. The posters were reprinted 2 years later when South Eastern became Connex.

FACING ABOVE The enduring British Rail 'Stop the Train' emergency alarm circa 1960, is still in use today on the Class 423 'slam-door' trains but is soon to be phased out.

FACING BELOW Practical signage from British Rail. Metal-cast handle instructions on the Class 423 'slam-door' trains, and information graphics from the British Railways Board Design Department.

BELOW A light-hearted yet earnest request from Swedish pop group Abba on behalf of British Rail, 1979.

Keep Your Station Tidy

locomotive design and the interiors of New York Central System's 20th Century Limited in 1935 resulted in what many rail historians consider a train and a service unsurpassed to date. But Dreyfuss's approach has been reinvented for the twenty-first century; the role of the marketing men in the corporate-identity process has created reams of brand-value appraisals, consumer-preference surveys and statistical analysis. In an increasingly competitive commercial world, risk assessment and crystal-ball-style predictions are essential to survival. It is not enough to rely on creative gut feeling or to trust the eye and expertise of the designer.

The history of design is invaluable in helping to inspire creativity, but it also illustrates how brand strategy and implementation can either stifle the persona of a company to such an extent that it loses direction, or nurture a company's identity back to life, with the aid of an imaginative and structured design process.

Creating an identity for a national rail service begins with policy. The British rail network's nationalization in 1948 amalgamated a few minor rail companies with 'The Big Four': the Great Western Railway (GWR), the London Midland & Scottish Railway (LMS), the London & North Eastern Railway (LNER) and the Southern Railway (SR). The disparateness of their existing liveries led to decades of identity crisis; moreover, the colour-coded regions of the new nationalized British Railways, added to the kaleidoscope of confusion. In addition to the indiscriminate allocation of maroon, orange, brown and pale blue, the British Transport Commission (the owners of British Railways) and the Railway Executive (the management) decided that they would each need a logo. The result was a pair of logotypes (dubbed 'hot dog' and 'starving lion') that not only had little visual commonality, but also led to a further dumbfounding of the customer-passenger.

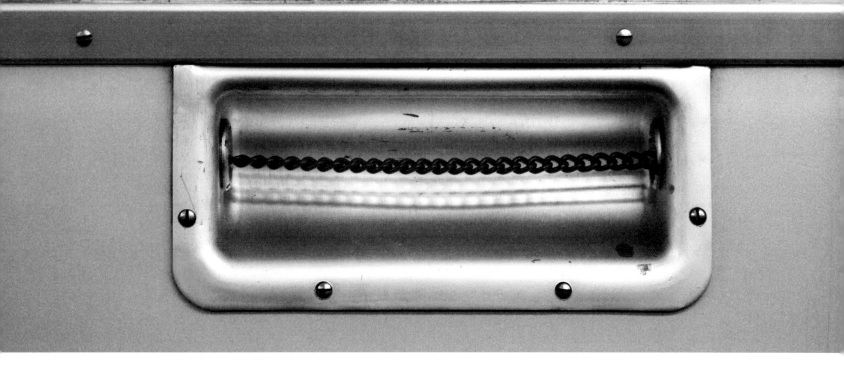

Alarm
Pull the chain
Penalty for improper use £50

The Second World War contributed greatly to the poor maintenance of rolling stock and the demise of services. Staff-recruitment prospects and public perception were at an all-time low, and the visual anomalies discussed were eclipsed by the all-consuming notion that Britain would never again see a rail service of which it could be proud. Post-war regeneration saw an increase in choice of other forms of transport. Planes, coaches and private automobiles competed with rail travel, prompting the British Railways Board to set up their Design Panel in 1956 to form a cohesive identity strategy. Detractors within the industry were gradually silenced as their work succeeded in winning back customers. The luxury diesel-electric Pullman was their first project, completed in 1959. They addressed all aspects of the design, from a new livery to interiors and cutlery, and further work on suburban services proved that good design leads to commercial success.

In 1965, in tandem with the British Government's initiative to make British Railways a profitable concern, the chairman of the newly formed British Railways Board, Dr Richard Beeching, unveiled a new corporate identity 'powerful enough to symbolize the service it stands for'. The scheme embraced everything, from rolling stock to uniforms, station architecture to publicity material. A team of design consultants, named Design Research Unit, founded by Misha Black and his partner Milner Gray, undertook the massive task. The two-way-traffic-arrow symbol, now so familiar, followed a number of graphic-design concepts that fell by the wayside, including a Union Jack flag incorporating the letters 'BR', and a reworking of the skinny, tongue-lolling lion that was inherited from the late 1940s.

The new British Rail logo was complemented by typographer Jock Kinneir's exquisitely executed Rail Alphabet. Based on Helvetica Medium, the typography was created for maximum legibility, aesthetics and fitness for purpose and its effectiveness was demonstrated through its use by other rail

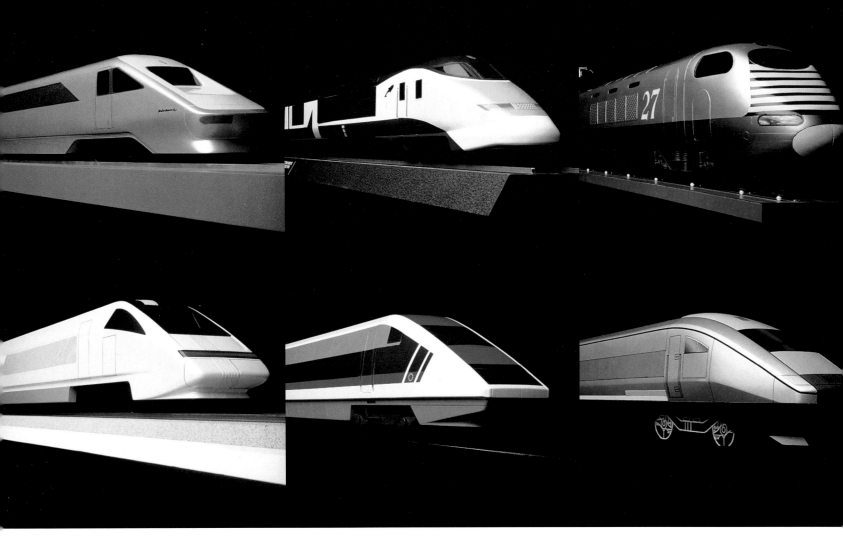

ABOVE Entries for the Channel
Tunnel Train Design Competition.
Designers were nominated by
each of the 3 national rail
companies involved with the route
that runs beneath the English
Channel to France and Belgium.
The winning entry was designed
by Jones Garrard of the UK.

LEFT After much research into
names, Eurostar was chosen over
other contenders such as
Albatross, EuroCity and The
Standing Express. The logo was
designed by Design Strategy in
Paris (later Minale Design
Strategy). Shown here are early
working visuals and the final
branding (SEE ALSO OVERLEAF).

FACING The original British Rail
Inter-City logo applied to the class
43 HST (High Speed Train) in the
1970s (ABOVE). The hyphen was
later removed from the Inter-City
logo in the attempt to convey a
little more confidence.
  Fresh branding: the 'swallow'
logo designed by Newell & Sorrell
in 1987 applied to an InterCity
125. The InterCity 125
inaugurated the world's fastest
diesel-powered rail services
in 1976.

tar

37 3214

Berlin-Warszawa-Express
PKP
615120-90 005-0 Böhmau

Amtrak

1
4

2
5

3
6

INTERCITY

ICE

SIEMENS

B

4322

43220
Bruxelles-Midi
Brussel-Zuid

THALYS

systems around the world. Fifteen years of consistent implementation followed the 1965 identity, which incorporated the symbol, the alphabet and the house colours, making British Rail one of the largest organizations ever to have attempted a total reformation of its image.

The political climate of the 1980s saw yet another change in rail policy as the government called for all areas of the British rail system to be financially self-sufficient. The British Railways Board decided to chop British Rail up into commercially viable bite-sized pieces. InterCity, Network SouthEast, Provincial, Railfreight and Parcels were each appointed a director to pursue and police profitability. In order to avoid visual chaos, the British Railways Board created a new design-overseer role, and in 1986 Jane Priestman was appointed Director of Architecture, Design & Environment. External corporate-identity consultants were also commissioned who, invested with the power to investigative all areas of British Rail, partly contributed to its eventual privatization. Design led to the restructuring of company operations and the task was immense. Tony Howard was Executive Design Manager: 'There were 40 people in the department, dealing with over 1,200 projects at any one time – from new trains and interiors to logos on socks. The corporate identity manual alone filled ten filing cabinets.' The results spoke for themselves as InterCity became the first profitable rail service in Europe and Railfreight enjoyed outstanding business success. The groundwork of successive internal design departments and external corporate-identity and product-design consultancies created some of the most innovative strategies and imaginative solutions for the British rail network, setting a global example of how branding and design can successfully launch ventures and change fortunes.

The most alluring aspect of rail travel today is that of 'the seamless journey'. The advantages of the train over other modes of mid-range travel are obvious. Even short-hop air routes can involve traffic-

FACING Applied livery: PKP was part of Polish State Railways until 2001. The limited company now runs the Berlin-Warsaw Express (in collaboration with Die Bahn) and the national Night Express sleepers (1); the logo used by Amtrak West business unit, 'Amtrak California' brand reflects the fact that much of their service is jointly funded (and in some cases operated) with the state of California (2); the Netherlands is served by Nederlands Spoorwegen (3); the InterCity 'swallow' logo designed by Newell & Sorrell in 1987 (4); Die Bahn's bold typographic solution for the high speed ICE service (5); the Belgian railway SNCB (6).

TOP AND ABOVE The French railway SNCF (Société Nationale des Chemins de Fer Français) was created in 1938. Seminal moments in recent history include the high-speed TGV Atlantique (September 1989), the TGV Nord-Europe (June 1993), and in collaboration with the Belgians and the British, the Eurostar service from Paris to London (November 1994).

FACING BELOW Thalys is a service provided jointly by the Belgian, French, Dutch and German railways.

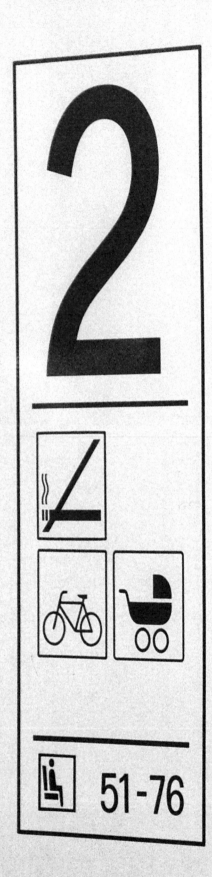

Graphics and hardware in harmony on Die Bahn's S-Bahn: The pictograms guide the passenger to the appropriate carriage with a clean and simple visual language (LEFT AND FACING ABOVE); the wide aisles and dedicated areas on board the S-Bahn can accommodate bicycles and prams with ease (FACING BELOW).

The LED information panel (ABOVE) on the exterior of the ICE 3 presents passenger information such as service number, coach number and destinations.

control congestion in the terminal, on the runway and at altitude, and congestion is also the bane of the freeway and Autobahn. The train journey begins at the first point of contact, say, advertising, and the branding consultant works on the total event, from start to finish.

A sea turtle, slowly finning its way through crystal-clear water – on initial consideration, this does not appear to be a particularly appropriate symbol for the identity of a high-speed rail service. However, this aquatic scene was Brent Oppenheimer's inspiration for the branding of Amtrak's Acela, the high-speed route serving America's Northeast Corridor, from Boston, via New York, to Washington DC. The Acela logo represents a sea turtle's fin, while the name Acela is suggestive of the words 'acceleration' and 'excellence'. Oppenheimer and partner Robin Haueter approached Amtrak and teamed up with design innovators IDEO to assist in the development of the new high-speed service. Moving away from the obvious advantages of high-speed rail travel as a fast way to get from A to B, their experiential approach to branding focused on this notion of 'the seamless journey' – a continuous, positive experience that starts long before the passenger steps on the train, and remains after the destination is reached.

The launch campaign, 'Life On Acela', created by DDB Needham, used a series of headlines that would not be amiss in a book of ancient Eastern philosophical teachings: 'Return your mind to its upright position', 'Depart from your inhibitions', and 'Inner children travel free'. The comfort theme was pursued throughout the remaining 'journey', with IDEO's flowing interiors reflecting a softer, more personal ambience than the hitherto standard rank-and-file layout. The environment on board suits both the leisure market and the higher proportion of business travellers. Seats, with lots of legroom, have audio sockets and electrical points for laptops. There are pay-phone areas for internet connection,

ABOVE Smart and casual: en route to Sacramento from Emeryville, California, an Amtrak conductor sports the current logo designed by OH&CO (ABOVE LEFT); at Ashford International Station, Kent, UK in 2004 a Eurostar passenger services team member wears a uniform designed by Jacqueline de Baer. The apparel is described as a 'non-uniform uniform' because of the informal, casual look. The dark-grey and charcoal uniforms, with yellow features, include beanie and baker boy's hats as well as wide winter scarves and polo shirts (ABOVE CENTRE); kepi and fleece – traditional mixes with practical modern for Belgian station staff (ABOVE RIGHT).

FACING an Amtrak conductor wears a cap bearing the Amtrak logo unkindly but accurately dubbed the 'Pointless Arrow'. The logo and accompanying corporate identity was designed in 1971 by Lippincott & Margulies (now Lippincott Mercer) who have also been responsible for branding corporate giants such as American Express, Coca-Cola and Chrysler.

numerous conference areas and a 'quiet' car for those seeking tranquillity. Automatic sliding glass panels separate vestibules from seating areas. The Acela Café offers the sort of fare that the discerning Bostonian or Manhattanite would expect. Some would argue that any rail journey is an experience, but the Acela experience confers convenience, personal time and, as Brent Oppenheimer explains, 'destination freedom' – a philosophy of giving the customer what they want, but also educating the traveller as to what is on offer and how to make the most of it. The Acela identity has been such a success that it has been applied to non-high-speed equipment on the Northeast Corridor, and Oppenheimer and Haueter's consultancy, OH&CO, is now managing the Amtrak brand nationwide with a challenge to 'Remake a federally created agency into a market-driven business'.

The rise in the number of airline passengers and the concomitant fall in that of rail travellers in America, from the late 1950s to the late 1960s, and the consequential decline of many railroads, resulted in the formation of the government-subsidized National Railroad Passenger Corporation in 1971, otherwise known as Amtrak. Decades of being a political football and of internal disagreement have obscured Amtrak's identity. The tide of perception is turning, however. As a result of the coordinated branding and design programme for Acela, there has begun a transformation in how Amtrak, their staff and their customers view rail travel. Acela could turn out to be the saviour of rail travel in the United States.

Historically, there have been certain notions as to what a train interior should look like. For decades, conservative design expectations and an unprogressive approach to manufacturing practices and use of materials have resulted in the train acquiring the image of an out-moded form of travel. Towards the end of the twentieth century, while architecture, furniture and commercial and domestic interiors were

LEFT Crew change on Amtrak's California Zephyr at Grand Junction, Colorado, April 2004. The brand identity designed by OH&CO in 2000, 'features a Travel Mark whose shape, convergent lines, and suggestion of movement capture the excitement of the travel experience', so states the corporate press release.

The logo and livery complement the powerful lines of a Genesis diesel-electric GE P42DC locomotive. The Genesis P40 was originally delivered in 1993 with the first order of P42s following in late 1996.

Industrial designer Cesar Vergara led Amtrak's design team on the Genesis following experience at Walter Dorwin Teague Associates and Henry Dreyfuss Associates, the founders of which created some of the most innovative steamliners of the 1930s.

ABOVE Amtrak's café car 6361 Angel Island carries the multiple arrows logo used by Amtrak West business unit. Sacramento, California, 2004.

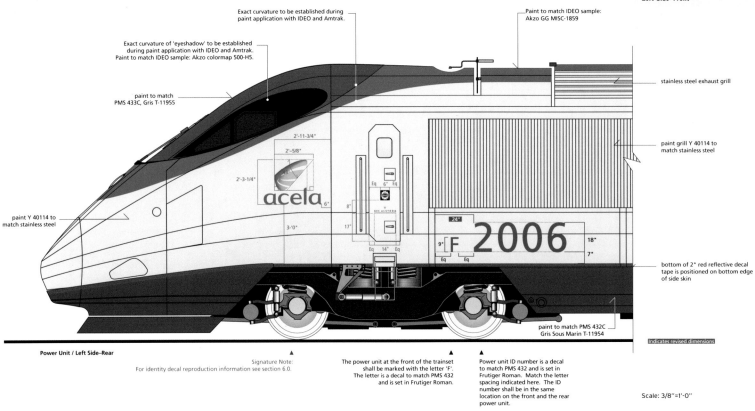

Exact curvature of 'eyeshadow' to be established during paint application with IDEO and Amtrak. Paint to match IDEO sample: Akzo colormap 500-H5.

Exact curvature to be established during paint application with IDEO and Amtrak.

Paint to match IDEO sample: Akzo GG MISC-1859

stainless steel exhaust grill

paint to match PMS 433C, Gris T-11955

paint grill Y 40114 to match stainless steel

paint Y 40114 to match stainless steel

bottom of 2" red reflective decal tape is positioned on bottom edge of side skin

paint to match PMS 432C Gris Sous Marin T-11954

Indicates revised dimensions

Power Unit / Left Side–Rear

Signature Note:
For identity decal reproduction information see section 6.0.

The power unit at the front of the trainset shall be marked with the letter 'F'. The letter is a decal to match PMS 432 and is set in Frutiger Roman.

Power unit ID number is a decal to match PMS 432 and is set in Frutiger Roman. Match the letter spacing indicated here. The ID number shall be in the same location on the front and the rear power unit.

Scale: 3/8"=1'-0"

The Acela Express, designed and supplied by Bombardier, serves Amtrak's high-speed route on America's Northeast Corridor, from Boston, via New York, to Washington DC.

The Acela logo represents a sea turtle's fin, while the name Acela is suggestive of the words 'acceleration' and 'excellence'. Brent Oppenheimer and partner Robin Haueter approached Amtrak and teamed up with design innovators IDEO to assist in the development of the new high-speed service. Moving away from the obvious advantages of high-speed rail travel as a fast way to get from A to B, their experiential approach to branding focused on this notion of 'the seamless journey' – a continuous, positive experience that starts long before the passenger steps on the train, and remains after the destination is reached. OH&CO's livery guidelines (FACING ABOVE); the icon system (FACING BELOW); the livery applied to locomotive and cars (RIGHT).

ABOVE The fresh and sophisticated launch campaign, 'Life On Acela', created by DDB Needham, used a series of headlines that would not be amiss in a book of ancient Eastern philosophical teachings: 'Return your mind to its upright position', 'Depart from your inhibitions', and 'Inner children travel free'.

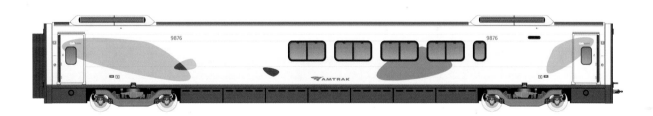

ABOVE Eiji Mitooka's sublime interiors for the Kamome express inaugurated in 2000 received the coveted Brunel Award, the highest honour in train-car design. In close collaboration with the Kyushu Railway Company and the engineers at Hitachi's Kasado Works, designer Eiji Mitooka and his team have developed unique interior, exterior and corporate identities for their whole fleet of trains.

FACING The Kamome word mark and logo are discreetly applied to the express locomotive. Between the headlights, the metal trophy, reminiscent of the Mercedes Benz 3-pointed star depicts the Kamome (sea bird).

enjoying inspired creative attention, train interiors struggled to keep pace. The 'tried and tested' school of design was answering the railway executives' briefs, but it was doing little to improve radically passenger patronage.

Alexander Neumeister is a pioneer in modifying rail companies' attitudes to the identity of their rolling stock. Neumeister is an archetypal industrial designer; his design ethos is socially responsible, yet innovative and ergonomic principles are key to his successful union of man and technology. His studio, in a converted piano showroom in a genteel part of Munich, has a Zen-like ambience, and the backlit parchment wall in the meeting room hints at his Far East connections. A graduate of the legendary Hochschule für Gestaltung (HfG) in Ulm, Germany, his train-design work has included a generation of high-speed trains for Die Bahn, numerous regional trains, the new Munich U-Bahn and the futuristic Maglev train for Transrapid International. In collaboration with the Japan West Railway Company and the Hitachi Design Team, Neumeister created the sensational exterior design for the Nozomi Series 500, which received the Minister of International Trade and Industry Prize in 1998, the first and only time that a foreigner has been awarded the national plaudit in Japan. He also worked with Hitachi engineer Morishige Hattori to develop the distinctive 15 metre (49 foot) nose of the Nozomi Express, resulting in one of the most striking Shinkansens in the Japanese landscape.

National identity is an important consideration in creating the experience that will attract the passenger. The high-speed Ave has revolutionized train travel in Spain. Seville, as host to the 1992 World Expo, was the first destination to be connected to the capital, Madrid, by the new service, and since its inception it has been a great success, cutting journey times between the two cities from six hours to two and a half and greatly increasing passenger numbers.

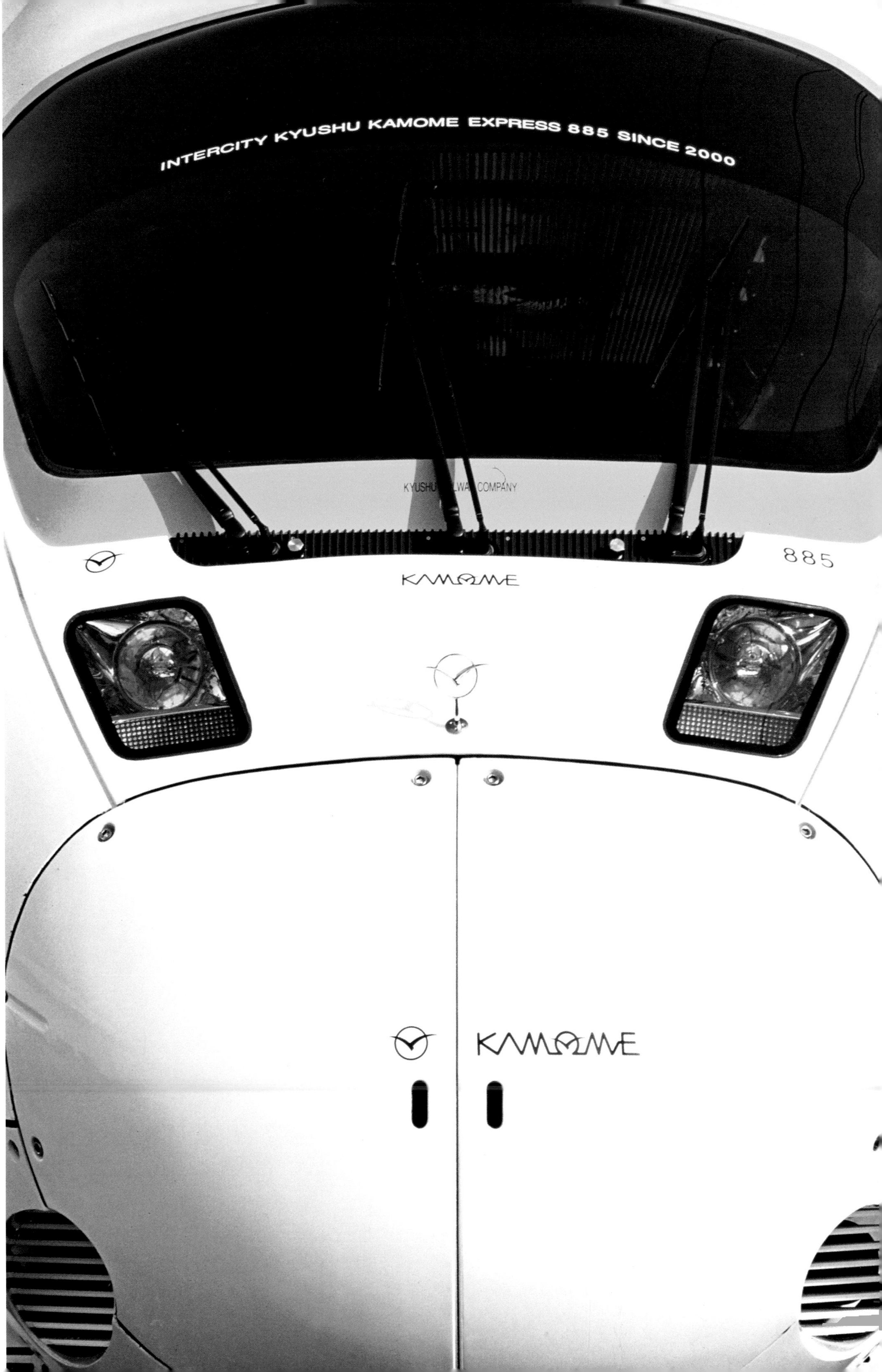
INTERCITY KYUSHU KAMOME EXPRESS 885 SINCE 2000
885
KAMOME
KAMOME

TSUBAME

The upgrading of the existing Madrid-to-Barcelona service required a slightly different approach to appeal to the high number of business commuters on the route. The director of Ave wanted his first-class accommodation to offer the same quality of service and environment as first-class passengers experience on intercontinental airline flights. Neumeister began by researching the social characteristics of potential passengers in Madrid and Barcelona. He visited art galleries, fashion stores, modern cafés and other public spaces, immersing himself in contemporary Spanish culture. The ICE 3, as used by Die Bahn, is the basis of the train, but that is where the similarity with the Siemens-built German vehicle ends. The Ave director's appraisal of the final result affirmed Neumeister's success at creating a very specific environment: 'This is a Spanish train!' National habits vary, and the Spanish prefer seat-service, so the cool, beechwood interior is complemented by stainless-steel strips, which protect furniture from damage by trolleys – a practical, yet attractive, solution. The area of the carriage behind the driver, which on the ICE 3 is reserved first-class or standard-class seating (depending on which direction you are travelling in), is a lounge, with glass boardroom table, surrounded by six executive-style chairs in black leather and polished aluminium. The effect has an air of exclusivity about it that is refreshingly unlike a train interior.

Ultimately, the successful identity is a cohesive union of innovative engineering and industrial design, universal informative graphics, sophisticated branding *and* a genuine culture of the best of passenger service – a rare but eminent combination.

つばめ

The ultimate identity for the ultimate train: The Shinkansen Tsubame is run by the Kyushu Railway Company. The Tsubame logo in English, the Tsubame Swallow symbol, headmark, Series 800 symbol and car number typography (FACING).

The Tsubame logo in Japanese (FAR LEFT).

The Tsubame's sleek white body with red and gold coach lines is complemented by the long nose. The roof (LEFT) features black and dark-red Japanese lacquer to re-create the colour of the swallow, referred to as 'tsubame'.

OVERLEAF Amtrak cars line up in almost perfect symmetry at Chicago's Union Station depot, Illinois, 2004.

Acknowledgements

A sincere thank you to Tony Howard, Brent Oppenheimer, Alexander Neumeister, David Notarius, Helen Slater, Alan Hegler, Don Heimburger, Karl Zimmermann and David Wright for their knowledge and enthusiasm.

With thanks to Laurence King, Jo Lightfoot, Felicity Awdry, Kerstin Peter, Laura Willis and Simon Cowell at Laurence King Publishing and a special thanks to Anne Townley for her guidance.

This book is dedicated to my father Edward Lovegrove.

I would like to thank the following people for their time and assistance:

David Wright, Edwin Renahan, Martyn Halman, Keira Méheux, Camilla Harrison and Helen Ashby (National Rail Museum, York); Ellen Halteman, Kathryn Santos, Stephen Drew, Paul Hammond and Susannah Willison (California State Railroad Museum); Keely Rennie-Tucker (Union Pacific Railroad Museum); Kurt Bell (Railroad Museum of Pennsylvania); Colin Nash, Colin Garratt (Milepost 92½); Tomohiro Totsuka (NHK); Venita Paul (Science & Society Picture Library); Ela Ginalska (Science Museum); Brenda Mainwaring (Union Pacific); Adam White, Adrian Berry (Factory Design); Kirsty Dias (Priestman Goode); Start Design; Glenn Adamson, Lauren Stevens (Brook Stevens); Charles Greenway, Phillip Lam (Atlantic Design); Yolaine Médélice (MBD Design); Didier Philippart, Misako Inoue (Cicero Translation); Alison Morgan (Dudson Museum, Staffordshire); Whitney Mortimer (IDEO); Brent Oppenheimer, John Kwo (OH&CO); Jones Garrard; Kellie Jackson, Karen MacLean (JR-Central); Amtrak Historical Society; Waldo Kopowski, Christiane Goecke (Die Bahn); Patrick Mueller, Walter Frei (Rhaetische Bahn); Jeremy Taylor, Gareth Headon (Eurostar); Ken Price, Michelle Malone (Palmer House Hilton, Chicago); Rail Gourmet; Railway Age; Marcello Minale, Alex Manzano (Minale Tattersfield Design Strategy); Jane Kennedy (Interbrand); DDB Needham; Christiane Frank (Neumeister+Partner Industrial Design); Bob Kennell, David Hancock (Canadian Pacific Railway Archive); Eiji Mitooka, Yoko Miura (Don Design Associates); Miki Yoshida (JR Kyushu Agency; Hitachi Rail; Transrapid International; Daniel Lopez (Amtrak); Sarah Swain (Amtrak Western Region); Marc Magliari, Stanley Jackson (Amtrak Central Region); Kyushu Railway Company; Museum of Science & Industry, Chicago; Rick Watson (Harry Ransom Research Center); Kathleen Mine (Thalys); Paul Flancbaum (ThyssenKrupp Budd); Lisa House (Raymond Loewy Foundation); The Bluebell Railway; Michael Johnson (Johnson Banks); Phil Gosney; David Werner; Momoko Williams; Richard Bowers; Jim Fullalove; Paul Hiscock; Anne Ransom; Paul Childs; John Sorrell; David Slater; W. David Randall; Phil and Bev Birk; Gary Schlerf; Bruce Hettema; Bill Gentle; Joe Welsh; Tom Garver; Richard Ganger; Catherine Bradley; Laurel Joseph; Nancy Lovegrove; Gilly Lovegrove; Simon Lince.

ABOVE Rush hour at Chicago's Union Station: passengers depart and arrive on Amtrak and Metra's bi-level stainless steel commuter cab-coach cars. 21st century arrival information displays the enduring influence of bygone nomenclature (FACING ABOVE).

TIME	TRAIN NAME	ORIGIN	DUE IN
10:30A	371 PERE MARQUETTE	Grand Rapids	11:00AM
10:35A	29 CAPITOL LIMITED	Washington DC	11:00AM
10:35A	348 ILLINOIS ZEPHYR	Quincy	10:45AM
10:50A	51 CARDINAL	New York	11:30AM
12:19P	334 HIAWATHA SERVICE	Milwaukee	ON TIME
12:26P	351 THE WOLVERINE	Pontiac	ON TIME
2:25P	22 TEXAS EAGLE	San Antonio	ON TIME
2:25P	322 TEXAS EAGLE	St Louis	ON TIME
2:29P	336 HIAWATHA SERVICE	Milwaukee	ON TIME
3:20P	4 SOUTHWEST CHIEF	Los Angeles	ON TIME
3:32P	6 CALIFORNIA ZEPHYR	Emeryville	4:32PM

Bibliography

Randall, W. David, and Anderson, William G., The Official Pullman-Standard Library Volume 13 Union Pacific Streamliners 1933-1937 (RPC Publications Inc, 1993)

Zimmermann, Karl, Domeliners: Yesterday's Trains of Tomorrow (Kalmbach Books, 1998)

Zimmermann, Karl, 20th Century Limited (MBI Publishing Company, 2002)

Heimburger, Donald J., and Byron, Carl R., The American Streamliner Prewar Years (Heimburger House Publishing Company, 1996)

Heimburger, Donald J., and Byron, Carl R., The American Streamliner Postwar Years (Heimburger House Publishing Company, 2001)

Garratt, Colin, The World Encyclopedia of Locomotives (Lorenz Books, 2002)

Burton, Anthony, The Rainhill Story (BBC, 1980)

Holland, Kevin J., The Streamliners (TLC Publishing, Inc., 2002)

Vincent, Mike, and Green, Chris, The InterCity Story (Oxford Publishing Company, 1994)

Freeman Allen, Geoffrey, Luxury Trains of the World (Bison Books Limited, 1979)

Alexander Neumeister/Designer Monographs 8 (Verlag form GmbH, 1999)

Hollingsworth, Brian, and Cook, Arthur, The Great Book of Trains (Salamander Books Limited, 1987)

Index

Page numbers in italics refer to captions to illustrations

"Acela Express" *114*, 143–4, *149*
Advanced Passenger Trains *see* APTs
AEG 57
"Aerolite" *122*
"Aerotrain" 131
Aitchison, Topeka & Santa Fe Railroad *37*, *43*, *105*, 129
Alco *16*, *19*, 25, 34, 48
Alsthom 64, 71
American Locomotive Company *see* Alco
Amtrak *43*, 46, 109–10, 116, *121*, *141*, 143–4, 147, 153
APTs 53, 64, 91
"Ariake Express" *70*
Art Deco style *16*, 34, *123*
"Atalanta" *123*
Atlantic class locomotives *19*, 25
Atlantic Design 55
"Avé" *104*, *150*, *152*

Baldwin Locomotive Works *16*, 25, 39, 55
Baltic locomotives 34
Baltimore & Ohio Railroad 34
Bauhaus style 34
Beeching Report 60
Bel Geddes, Norman *16*, 55
Bennie, George 56
"Bernina Express" *59*
"Blackmoor Vale" *122*
"Blue Pullman" 60, 64
branding 121, *123*, 125, 131–2, 134, *147*, 149
"Brighton Belle " *103*
British Rail (formerly British Railways) 53, 64, *91*, *105*, 110,

133, 136, *137*, 141
British Railways (later British Rail) 60, 64, *83*, *106*, *129*, *133*, 134, 136
Budd, Ralph 20
Budd Company *19*, 20, 39, 105
Bulleid, Oliver 48
Bulleid Light Pacific locomotives *122*
Bulleid Pacific locomotives 48
bullet trains *see* Shinkansen trains
Burlington Northern Railroad *99*, *126*
"Burlington Zephyr" *20*, 39, *43*, 123

"California Zephyr" *43*, 46, *85*, 109, 116, *147*
"Camelot" 125
Canadian National Railroad *131*
Canadian Pacific Railroad *29*, *34*, *41*, *43*, *59*, *96*, 131
cars and carriages *11*, *19*, *20*, 74
"Alexander" *13*
"Angel Island" *147*
buffet cars 48, *53*
Chateau series *41*
coach-baggage cars *13*
decor *4*, *22*, *31*, *34*, *43*, *51*, *70*, *72*, *152*
"Delmonico" *92*
dining cars *72*, *74*, *92*, *96*, *105*, 111, 116
"Green" carriage *13*
lounge cars *25*, *31*, *34*, *37*, *43*
Manor series *41*
"Mokelumne River" *121*
observation cars *25*, *34*, *43*, *105*, 116
parlor cars *22*
"President" *92*
Pullman cars *13*, 26, *31*–2

recreation cars *85*
"Royal Saloon" *48*
"Sacramento Valley" *121*
sleeping cars 26, *32*, *39*, *41*, *53*, *64*, 110
smoking lounges 26
"Superliner Deluxe" *110*
tavern cars *22*
see also facilities
"Catch Me Who Can" 11
Central Japan Railway Company *see* JR Central
Central Transportation Company 26
"Challenger Domeliner" *37*
Channel Tunnel *11*, 137
Chicago, Alton & St. Louis Railroad 92
Chicago, Burlington & Quincy Railroad *20*, 39, *43*, 123
Chicago, Milwaukee, St. Paul & Pacific Railroad *see* Milwaukee Road
Chicago, Rock Island and Pacific Railroad *126*
Chicago & North Western Railroad 32
china *96*, *105*, 110
"Cisalpino" *104*
"City of Denver" *22*, *31*
"City of Los Angeles" *31*, *32*, 116
"City of Miami" *93*
"City of San Francisco" *32*, *43*
Class 423 'slam-door' trains *134*
combustion-powered locomotives *31*, 57
Connex *134*
Cooper, Jack 64, 71
Coronation class, Pacific locomotives 55
"Côte d'Azur Express" *123*
Cret, Paul *16*, *20*, 39, 55, *123*

De Witt Clinton locomotives 25
Delaware & Hudson Railroad 55
Deltic locomotives 50, 60, *121*
"Denver Zephyr" *22*
Design Research Unit *133*, 136
Deutsche Reichsbahn 25
"Devon Belle" *83*
Die Bahn 56, *69*, *74*, *141*, *142*, *150*
diesel-electric locomotives *7*, 39, *43*, 46, 60, 66, *121*, 136
diesel locomotives 20, *31*, 64, *137*
"Doctor Yellow" *75*
"Domeliner" *59*, 131
domeliner trains *37*, *59*, *105*, 116, 125, *131*
Dreyfuss, Henry *16*, *43*, 48, 51, 132, 134
"Duchess of Gloucester" *14*, 55

E-Series trains 60
E9a locomotives *7*
"Edith" *123*
800-Series trains *4*, *70*, *72*, *153*
"El Capitan" *37*, *43*, *105*, 129
electric trains 55, 57, 64, 66, 71–2, 78
emergency alarms *134*
"Empire Builder" 26, *37*, *99*
English Electric 60, *121*
Eurostar *11*, 71, *104*, *106*, 131–2, *137*, *141*, *158*
"Excalibur" 125

F-Series trains 60
facilities
bars *22*, *34*, *83*
for communication *72*, *74*, 143
on El Capitan *43*
food *83*, *86*, *92*, 97–104, *105*–11, *114*–15, 116, 144
movies 26, *72*, *85*

in Pullman cars 31
on 20th Century Limited 51
trolley service 83, 86, 89, 114
on Virgin trains 66
washrooms 37, 70, 72
see also cars and carriages
Feather River Route, Scenic Limited
126
films using trains 4, 26, 39
500-Series trains 64, 75, 93, 150
"Fliegende Zuege" 25
"Florida Special" 85
Flugbahngesellschaft 25

General Motors 7, 20, 31, 39, 60,
125, 126, 131
Genesis locomotives 147
GG-1 locomotives 55
"God of the West Wind" 39, 123
"Golden Arrow" 48
Great Central Railway 96
Great Eastern Railway 92, 100
Great Northern Railway 26, 37, 99,
121
Great Western Railway (GWR) 48,
89, 110, 112, 122, 134
Great Western Railway of Canada
92
Gresley, Sir Nigel 55, 69

Hattori, Morishige 150
Haueter, Robin *see* OH&CO
headboards 48, 50
"Heidi Express" 59
Hiawatha trains 19, 25, 126
high-speed rail travel 25, 56, 57,
64, 72, 75, 78, 143
Hill, James Jerome 99
history of rail travel 57, 60
    America 25–6, 31–2, 39, 43, 48,
    51, 55, 92, 97

Britain 11, 16, 20, 25, 55, 60, 64,
100
Europe 25, 55, 57, 64, 71, 100,
104
Japan 61, 72, 78
Hitachi 64, 150
Holabird & Root 20, 39, 123
Howard, Tony 53, 141
Hudson locomotives 16, 48, 51

I-5 class locomotives (Shore Liners)
16
ICE trains 56, 69, 71–2, 74, 104,
106, 141, 142, 152
IDEO 143, 149
Illinois Central Railroad 7, 22, 93
Indian trains 111, 114, 116
Inter City Express trains *see* ICE
trains
InterCity trains 53, 64, 105, 110,
137, 141

J-1 class, Baltic locomotives 34
J-3a class, Hudson locomotives 16
Japanese National Railway 72, 75
Jones Garrard 137
JR Central 75, 78, 93, 114
JR West 61, 64, 69

K-4 & K-5 class, Pacific
locomotives 19, 39, 43, 48
"Kamome Express" 150
Kemper, Hermann 56
Kettering, Charles 20
KF1-7 class locomotives 11
King Arthur class locomotives 125
"King Victor Emmanuel" 121
Kinneir, Jock 133, 136, 141
Kruckenberg, Franz 25, 57
Kuhler, Otto 16, 19, 34, 39, 57, 60
Kyushu Railway Company 4, 70,

72, 91, 114, 150, 153

Lacroix, Christian 78
Lehigh Valley Railroad 39
Lima Locomotive Works 25
Liverpool & Manchester Railway 11,
16
livery 134
    Amtrak 147, 149
    Atlantic class 19
    Canadian National Railway 131
    Deltic locomotives 121
    Eurostar 131–2
    GG-1 locomotives 55
    Illinois Central 93
    LMS (Crimson Lake) 14
    "Train of Tomorrow" 125
    "Tsubame Express" 153
    "20th Century Limited" 51
    Victorian 121, 123
Loewy, Raymond 16, 19, 55
logos
    "Acela Express" 143, 149
    Amtrak 121, 141, 143, 147, 149
    British Rail 133, 137
    British Railways 133, 134, 136
    Canadian National Railway 131
    Canadian Pacific Railroad 131
    Eurostar 137, 158
    GWR 122
    Hiawatha 126
    InterCity 137, 141
    "Kamome Express" 150
    LNER 122
    Milwaukee Road 126
    New York Central System 126
    Northern Pacific Railroad 126
    "The Pan-American" 126
    Pennsylvania Railroad 126
    Rock Island Railroad 126
    Scenic Limited 126

"Tsubame Express" 153
    Union Pacific Railroad 126
    Wabash Railroad 126
    Western Pacific Railroad 126
London & Birmingham Railway 50
London & North Eastern Railway
    (LNER) 55, 56, 112, 121, 122,
    123, 134
London & North Western Railway
    50, 89
London Midland & Scottish Railway
    (LMS) 14, 50, 55, 103, 112, 134
Louisville & Nashville Railroad 126

M-10000 trains 31
magnetic levitation (Maglev) 56,
64, 75, 78
"Mallard" 55, 69
MBD Design 78
Merchant Navy class locomotives
48
"The Mercury" 43, 48
Miller, Terry 64
Milwaukee Road 19, 25, 126
Minale Design Strategy 131, 132,
137
Mitooka, Eiji 150
Mk 1, 2a & 3b trains 53
Mohawk & Hudson Railroad 25
monorails 56
Monterey & Salinas Valley Railroad
13

Nagelmackers, Georges 32, 34, 100,
104
nameplates 121, 122
Nederlands Spoorwegen 141
Neumeister, Alexander 56, 64, 71,
150, 152
New York, New Hampshire and
Hartford Railroad 16

ABOVE The final resting place: redundant railway carriages converted to provide holiday accommodation were introduced in 1933. The relatively low rent of about £3 ($5) a week made them popular and by 1935 there were over 200 located at various holiday destinations across the UK. Here, a family listens to their portable record player. Cheddar Station, Somerset, UK, 1951.

New York Central System *16, 26, 34, 43, 48, 51, 126, 134*
noise 71, *74*
"Norfolk Coast Express" *100*
North Eastern Railway 83, *122*
Northern Pacific Railroad 55, *100, 126*
"Nozomi Express" *64, 93, 150*
numbered locomotives
5926 (Canadian Pacific) *29*
4034 (Illinois Central) *7*

OH&CO 143, 144, 147, *149*
100-Series trains *69*
Oppenheimer, Brent *see* OH&CO
"Orient Express" *32, 104*
"Oriental Limited" *37*

Pacific locomotives *19, 39, 43, 48, 55*
"Palatino" *104*
"The Pan-American" *126*
"Panama Limited" *22*
Paris, Lyon and Mediterranean Railway *123*
Pennsylvania Railroad *19, 55, 97, 126*
"Penydarren" *11*
"Pioneer" *31*
PKP *141*
posters *48, 105, 110, 112, 124, 129, 134*
Priestman, Jane *141*
"Princess Royal" *123*
Problem-class locomotives *121, 123*
"Puffing Devil" *11*
Pullman, George Mortimer 26, 31, *92*
Pullman Palace Car Company *13, 26, 31, 48*
Pullman-Standard Car

Manufacturing Company *22, 31, 32, 51, 93*

"Queen Guinevere" *125*
"Queen of Scots" *50*

"Rail Zeppelin" *25, 57*
railplanes *56*
Rainhill Trials *11, 16, 20*
"Rajdhani Express" *111, 116*
"Rak 3" *57*
"Relay Tsubame Express" *91*
Rhaetische Bahn *59*
Rock Island Railroad *126*
"The Rocket" *11, 16, 20*
"Rome Express" *100*
"Royal Blue" *34*
"Royal Scot" *14*
royal trains *48, 50*

S-1 class locomotive ("American Railroads") *55*
S-Bahn trains *142*
Scenic Limited, Western Pacific Railroad *126*
"Schienenzeppelin" *25, 57*
"Schneeschleudern" *59*
Seaboard Air Line *131*
Seaboard Coast Line *85*
seating *53, 55, 70, 71, 75, 78, 152*
700-Series trains *70, 75, 91, 93*
SFAI (Societa' Ferroviaria dell'Alta Italia) *121*
Shanghai Transrapid *56*
Shinkansen trains (bullet trains) *4, 61, 64, 72, 75, 93, 111, 150, 153*
Siemens *57, 72, 152*
signs *122, 134, 142, 149*
"Silver Star," "Silver Comet" & "Silver Meteor" *131*
"Sir Lancelot" *125*

SNCB (Belgian Railways) *141*
SNCF (French Railways) *4, 64, 78, 105, 141*
"Sonic Express" *72*
Soo Line *126*
South Eastern Railway *134*
South West Trains *55*
Southern Pacific Line *114*
Southern Railway (SR) *48, 86, 110, 112, 122, 125, 134*
Southern Region (British Railways) *83, 129*
staff
catering staff *86, 96, 97, 99, 100, 103*
conductors *86, 89, 144*
engineers *86*
firemen *14*
guards *89*
porters *86, 93*
Purserettes *91*
stewards/stewardesses *85, 86, 91, 93, 96, 106, 114*
Zephyrettes *85*
Stanier, Sir William *55*
Starck, Philippe *132*
steam locomotives *4, 10, 11, 16, 20, 25, 55, 60, 123*
Stephenson, Robert *11, 16, 20, 25*
Stevens, Brook *25, 55*
"Stirling No. 1" *121*
Stockton & Darlington Railway *13*
streamliners *16, 19, 31, 34, 39, 55, 57, 60, 123*
"Sunrise Express" *64*
"Super Chief" *105*

Teague, Walter Dorwin *16, 51*
Terre Haute, Alton & St. Louis Railroad *26*
TGVs *64, 71, 78, 104, 141*

Thalys 104, *141*
300-Series trains *75*
tilting trains *72, 104*
"Tokaido Express" *61*
"Train of Tomorrow" *125*
Trains á Grande Vitesse *see* TGVs
Trans-Canada Limited *86, 96*
"Trans-Europe Express" *60*
"Trans-Siberian Express" *32*
Transrapid 07 train *56*
Transrapid International *78, 150*
Trevithick, Richard *11*
"Tsubame Express" *4, 70, 91, 153*
"20th Century Limited" *16, 26, 48, 51, 134*
232U class locomotives *4*

Union Pacific Railroad *22, 31, 32, 34, 37, 105, 116, 126*
Union Station, Chicago *83, 117, 153*

Vergara, Cesar *147*
Victorian trains *11, 20, 25, 92, 121*
Virgin Trains *66, 86*
von Opel, Fritz *57*

Wabash Railroad *126*
Wagon-Lits *32, 100, 104*
wartime trains *112*
Water Level Route, New York Central System *16, 48*
Wenner-Gren, Dr Axel Lennart *56*
West Point Foundry *25*
Western Pacific Railroad *85, 126*
Woodruff, Theodore Tuttle *26*
Wrightson, Keith *53*

X2000 trains *104*
XP64 trains *53*

"Zébulon" *64*